Praise for *Good Poems for Hard Times*

"If I could choose only one book to give every inhabitant of post-Katrina New Orleans, it would be Garrison Keillor's remarkable and wide-ranging collection of *Good Poems for Hard Times*. What a lovely, consoling book, perfect reading for these days when everyone is struggling with something . . . the 185 poems in this collection do help."
    —*The Times-Picayune* (New Orleans)

"Irresistible."
    —*The Arizona Republic*

"[Keillor's] taste is excellent. . . . [H]e knows good poetry."
    —*Booklist*

By Garrison Keillor

The Book of Guys

A Christmas Blizzard

Good Poems

Good Poems, American Places

Good Poems for Hard Times

Guy Noir and the Straight Skinny

Happy to Be Here

Homegrown Democrat

The Keillor Reader

Lake Wobegon Days

Lake Wobegon Summer 1956

Leaving Home

Liberty

Love Me

Pilgrims

Pontoon

We Are Still Married

Wobegon Boy

GOOD POEMS

for Hard Times

Selected and Introduced by

GARRISON KEILLOR

PENGUIN BOOKS

PENGUIN BOOKS

Published by the Penguin Group

Penguin Group (USA) Inc., 375 Hudson Street, New York, New York 10014, U.S.A.

Penguin Group (Canada), 90 Eglinton Avenue East, Suite 700, Toronto,
Ontario, Canada M4P 2Y3 (a division of Pearson Penguin Canada Inc.)

Penguin Books Ltd, 80 Strand, London WC2R 0RL, England

Penguin Ireland, 25 St Stephen's Green, Dublin 2, Ireland (a division of Penguin Books Ltd)

Penguin Group (Australia), 250 Camberwell Road, Camberwell,
Victoria 3124, Australia (a division of Pearson Australia Group Pty Ltd)

Penguin Books India Pvt Ltd, 11 Community Centre, Panchsheel Park, New Delhi–110 017, India

Penguin Group (NZ), 67 Apollo Drive, Rosedale, North Shore 0632, New Zealand
(a division of Pearson New Zealand Ltd)

Penguin Books (South Africa) (Pty) Ltd, 24 Sturdee Avenue,
Rosebank, Johannesburg 2196, South Africa

Penguin Books Ltd, Registered Offices:
80 Strand, London WC2R 0RL, England

First published in the United States of America by Viking Penguin,
a member of Penguin Group (USA) Inc. 2005
Published in Penguin Books 2006

21 23 25 27 29 30 28 26 24 22

Pages 339–344 constitute an extension of this copyright page.

THE LIBRARY OF CONGRESS HAS CATALOGED THE HARDCOVER EDITION AS FOLLOWS:
Good poems for hard times / selected and introduced by Garrison Keillor.
p. cm.
Includes index.
ISBN 0-670-03436-3 (hc.)
ISBN 978-0-14-303767-5 (pbk.)
1. American poetry.   2. English poetry.   I. Keillor, Garrison.
PS586.G59 2005
811.008—dc22   2005042316

Printed in the United States of America

To the English teachers of America,
doing good work every day,
with admiration and affection
from an old student

Contents

3. THIS LUST OF TENDERNESS

4. DELIBERATE OBFUSCATION

5. THE SOUND OF A CAR

9. I FEEL OUR KINSHIP

10. SIMPLER THAN I COULD FIND WORDS FOR

Introduction

Back when I was your age and had much too much time on my hands, I was ambitious to be a poet and even went so far as to write a few poems and send them away to magazines, double-spaced, with a stamped envelope. The poems were full of passionate obscurity; they veered between whimsy and nihilism; and they sounded like bad translations of, say, a gloomy Swede who'd never left Göteborg, and yet, being 21 and confident of my calling, I felt validated by the magazines' rejection of them and could have gone on writing the stuff for years and years. What killed my career was encouragement. I wrote a poem called "Crucifixion" and a friend of mine (himself a poet) wrote me a letter praising it that only made me see how cheap and fraudulent it was and I didn't want to be that kind of fake. I made a simple moral decision: it is probably better to imitate humor than portentous despair. I quit cold turkey. Aside from the occasional limerick for somebody's birthday, I've been clean ever since.

As a grad student in English, I wrote long, heavily ornamented, semi-intelligible papers about Milton and Yeats and Matthew Arnold whose sheer density amazes me today. (The writer of those papers knew less about life than Einstein knew about the Delta blues.) But my most intense and authentic experience of poetry was stealing the *Oxford Anthology of Verse* from Dayton's department store in downtown Minneapolis when I was 16. It was a lovely big book and I opened it, inhaled the pages, let temptation burgeon and simmer, and since the Dayton's sales personnel were occupied with Christmas customers, I stuffed the book under my jacket and walked out on Eighth Street and turned right, toward Hennepin, and thought, *You should go to jail for this*, and walked along at a good clip, half-expecting a big claw to clamp on to my shoulder. I hid the book in my bedroom and concocted a story about a kind stranger who had given it to me ("Here, son. Once when I was your age, a man gave me a book of poems that changed my life, and now I am repeating the favor."), which seemed pretty flimsy, and then I got an inspiration. I gave the book to Dad for Christmas. He was surprised: a rather opulent gift from a kid on a small allowance. Dad was a railway mail clerk and carpenter and his taste in poetry ran toward Longfellow, toward hymns and exhortations to faith and to labor, and it stopped short at the door of modernism. Dad was not a questioner of the faith and he had no time for skeptics and when he saw how much skepticism there was in the *Oxford Anthology* he abandoned it and it migrated to my room. I lay up there, reading Frost and Cummings and Sandburg and Eliot, stolen pleasures to me now, for which I had risked arrest, prosecution, a year in the reformatory at Red Wing, shame to my family, the end of my hopes of college, the beginning of a lifetime of menial jobs. I had risked all of that, just as the boy in Frost's poem risks life and limb to swing on the birch tree. Just as Adam and Eve ate from the apple in disobedience to Divine instruction—a necessary sin, humankind not meant to remain as children in the nursery Garden but meant by God to live real lives.

That was my last theft. (You only need to bite the apple once.) A few years later, I made restitution to the Daytons, a good Presbyterian clan whose beneficence to the community was well known. I came to love that book that I had risked so much for and taken my conscience into my own hands. Poetry is a necessity as simple as the need to be touched and similarly a need that is hard to enunciate. The intense vision and high spirits and moral grandeur are simply needed lest we drift through our days consumed by clothing options and hair styling and whether to have the soup or the salad.

The meaning of poetry is to give courage. A poem is not a puzzle that you the dutiful reader are obliged to solve. It is meant to poke you, get you to buck up, pay attention, rise and shine, look alive, get a grip, get the picture, pull up your socks, wake up and die right. Poets have many motives for writing (to be published on expensive paper, to show up the others in your M.F.A. program, to flaunt your sensitive nature and thereby impress someone who might then go to bed with you, to win valuable prizes and fellowships and maybe a year in Rome or Provence, to have a plausible excuse for making a mess of your life), but what really matters about poetry and what distinguishes poets from, say, fashion models or ad salesmen is the miracle of incantation in rendering the gravity and grace and beauty of the ordinary world and thereby lending courage to strangers. This is a necessary thing. At times life becomes almost impossible, and you curl up under a blanket in a dim room behind drawn shades and you despise your life, which seems mean and purposeless, a hoax and a cheat, your shining chances all wasted, pissed away, nobody can change this or make this better, love is lost, hope gone, nothing left but to pour a glass of gin and listen to weepy music. But it can help to say words. Moaning helps. So does prayer. God hears prayer and restores the souls of the faithful. Walking helps. Many people have pulled themselves up out of the pit by the simple expedient of rising to their feet, leaning slightly forward, and putting one foot ahead of the other. Poems help. In Mrs. Fleischman's eleventh-grade English class, my assignment was to memorize Shakespeare's sonnet "When in disgrace with fortune and men's eyes," and so I did, and having it in my head for forty years has brought me many moments of clarity, and also Housman's "Loveliest of trees the cherry now," and "A Blessing" by James Wright, and "Wild Geese" by Mary Oliver (both in *Good Poems*, the predecessor to this book) and other poems. They don't come to me in moments of hilarity, but often when feeling bereft or drowning in work or even just being *late* to an appointment, stuck in traffic, ranting at myself, Wright's two Indian ponies have come to me, their eyes full of kindness, Oliver's geese have honked, Shakespeare's lark at break of day from sullen earth arises, the heart is calmed, the gnashing stops, and one goes on.

America is in hard times these days, the beloved country awash to the scuppers in expensive trash, gripped by persistent jitters, politics even more divorced from reality than usual, the levers of power firmly in the hands of a cadre of Christian pirates and bullies whose cynicism is stunning, especially their perversion of the gospel of the Lord to blast the poor and the meek and subvert the tax system in favor of the rich, while public institutions are put into perpetual fiscal crisis, meanwhile newspapers dwindle in sad decline, journalism is lost in the whirlwind of amusement, and the hairy hand of the censor reaches out—what mustn't be lost, in this dank time, is the passion of young people for truth and justice and liberty—the spirit that has kept the American porch light lit through dark ages of history—and when this spirit is betrayed by the timid and the greedy and the naive, then we must depend on the poets. American poetry is the truest journalism we have. What your life can be, lived bravely and independently, you can discover in poetry.

People complain about the obscurity of poetry, especially if they're assigned to write about it, but actually poetry is rather straightforward compared to ordinary conversation with people you don't know well, which tends to be jumpy repartee, crooked, coded, allusive to no effect, firmly repressed, locked up in irony, steadfastly refusing to share genuine experience—think of conversation at office parties or conversation between teenage children and parents, or between teenagers themselves, or between men, or between bitter spouses: rarely in ordinary conversation do people speak from the heart and mean what they say. How often in the past week did anyone offer you something from the heart? It's there in poetry. Forget everything you ever read about poetry, it doesn't matter—poetry is the last preserve of honest speech and the outspoken heart. All that I wrote about it as a grad student I hereby recant and abjure—all that matters about poetry to me now is directness and clarity and truthfulness. All that is twittery and lit'ry: no thanks, pal. A person could perish of entertainment, especially comedy, so much of it casually nihilistic, hateful, glittering, cold, and in the end clueless. People in nursing homes die watching late-night television and if I were one of them, I'd be grateful when the darkness descends. Thank God if the pastor comes and offers a psalm and a prayer, and they can attain a glimmer of clarity at the end.

My dad and I were as different as could be (I made sure of that), but his life had a clarity that I find in poetry. He was a carpenter, and if I close my eyes, I can see him, thirtyish, handsome, sawdust in his dark hair, running a 2x4 through a circular saw, trimming it, holding it up to the studs, pulling a nail out from between his front teeth, taking the hammer from the loop on his pants where it hung, and pounding in the nail, three whacks, and a tap for good luck. This simple act, repeated a thousand times as he built the house up over our heads, had the cadence and fervor of poetry. He didn't earn his daily bread sitting in a conference room, manipulating people, moving big wads of cash around, spinning a web of hogwash: compared to that, his life was poetry. When he bowed his head and gave thanks before a meal, it was always the same words, the same cadence. When he took a chicken by the legs and laid its neck against the block and lifted the ax and chopped off its head, there was a plain cadence to that. I hear that *whack* in poetry. Comedians are the children at the upstairs window, amused by the hysteria of chickens trying to escape over the fence, waiting for the hammerer to pound his thumb so they can imitate his pain, hop around and howl. Comedy is a predatory sport, closer to the lynch mob than to church. Poetry is church. What animates poetry is faith, the same faith that moves the builder and the butcher. My dad died in the first-floor bedroom of the house he built and his death had a plain cadence to it. When I brought my three-year-old daughter to see him two weeks before he died, he wriggled his toes under the blanket to make her reach for them and then he withdrew them to make her giggle. He had been making children giggle all his life. His voice and the heat of his life can be found in poetry and nowhere else: poetry is about driving the nail into the pine, killing the chicken, mowing grass, putting luggage into the car, gratitude for food, the laughter of a little girl, about our common life.

The common life is precarious. I fear a future in which America becomes a loose aggregate of marauding tribes—no binding traditions, no songs that we all know, not even "The Star-Spangled Banner" or "Silent Night," no common heroes, no American literature—only the promotional lit of race and ethnicity, our people unable to name their senators, their only political experience via television, their only public life at Wal-Mart. There are no more TV shows that everyone knows: 10 percent of audience is a huge hit. The last singer recognizable to everyone was Frank Sinatra, the last poet known far and wide was Robert Frost. There are no replacements in sight. Today's celebrities are people whom most Americans haven't heard of. Our culture—jazz, especially, and movies—once united us, a point of pride, uniquely American, but school boards are slaughtering arts education on every hand—programs are dead or dying that used to bus kids to hear an orchestra or see a play—children are cheated out of poetry and French and the cello—meanwhile, interscholastic football, the great passion of unhappy men, grows by leaps and bounds, and children are conditioned for the passive life in which commercial trademarks become their insignia here in the United Corporations of America. You lie in a hotel bed at night, remote in hand and surf a hundred channels of television, Weather, Golf, History, Shopping, Food, Disney, Rerun, Rerun 2 and 3, Cartoons, Movie, News, Fox News, and you can drift for hours among the flotsam and you will never see anything that shows that you're in Knoxville or Seattle or Santa Fe or Chicago and nobody will ever speak to you as straightforwardly and clearly as poetry does. Nobody. They don't even try. You can lie in that bed for a week, getting sicker and sicker, waiting to hear one daring and heartfelt word, and it will not come. Everything is slicker than catshit in the moonlight, the clammy sincerity of anchor persons, the shallow knowingness on all sides, the beloved sheepdip of commercials, the clumsy cunning of politicians, incessant flacking and spinning and winking and preening and strutting, but if you're looking for plain passionate speech, you won't find it there—now and then, on a soap opera, a character may utter a meaningful line ("Why can't you let me love you, Richard?") and sometimes a preacher comes out with a good thought ("Think not of the morrow.") but television is a product, not a medium, and everything you see and hear is produced by people terrified that they might be banished from the castle tomorrow and lose their limos and expense-account lunches and become peasants again, so there is mighty little courage or playfulness, as there is in poetry, which is entirely created by peasants, every word. Banishment is a way of life for poets, so what's to be afraid of?

Poetry is free speech. It is ever on the side of the irrepressible spirit and in opposition to the censor, to Management, to the protocols of the company psychologist, to the roomful of men in blue suits who casually cheat schoolchildren. It is on the side of exhilaration and the stupendous vision, the sight of the stars through the barred window, the perfection of small birds, the democracy of their chittering language and of our own yakfest and hullabaloo. Poetry is made of the grandeur that is available to a man with no fortune but with somewhere to walk to and ears to hear and a mind to transport him. He may be defeated in love and finance and yet the night belongs to him, he feels entrusted with the stunning sky, the guardian of the houses on the street and all the people in them. So are poets, the angels and shepherds of the sleeping world.

The intensity of poetry, its imaginative fervor, its cadences, is not meant for the triumphant executive, but for people in a jam—you and me. Remember the last time you hitchhiked and stood, thumb out, as the cars whooshed past, waiting for the kind stranger, focusing on each pair of oncoming headlights and thinking, *I am not a killer. I won't weird you out. I am actually extremely nice. I am a student in college. I really need you to stop and give me a ride.* Then your hitchhiking days were over. You graduated. You got a good job, a car, a family, a house, a church, you salted away some dough. And then trouble struck. (Sirens, klaxons, cries of alarm.) And now, *damn it*, you are (figuratively) right back out there on the highway, except now it's raining. Maybe your good job went up in smoke. Perhaps your assets have been turned to succotash by a lousy investment in an old warehouse you meant to convert to fashionable shops and ethnic restaurants, which you halfway did and then it went belly up, there being too many such warehouses in your town, and an accountant in a blue-striped shirt gives you the plain bad news, and now you may lose your lovely old 1910 manse under the elms with the bay window and curved veranda on the big corner lot in Crocus Hill, and now you must scrabble your way back up the slippery slope again, but you're older and less steady and your heart sinks at the prospect of having to grind out a living again. Perhaps you have gotten a terrible phone call from your beautiful faraway child—liver cancer? How can a kid get liver cancer? She's 34 and lovely and exercises daily and never drank or smoked!—and now your good life is upheaved, time is stopped and the calendar canceled, and you're off on the plane to a hospital drama in a strange city. Perhaps your brother, the one you've worried about for twenty years, has finally gone careening off the road at 3 A.M. and totaled his car and is still firmly in denial that his drinking must now be discussed though his wife is in torment and his children wary and confused and you must face him and be the recipient of his stupid anger. These troubles come to people all the time. —Perhaps you are foundering on work and no help is at hand.

Me, too. —Perhaps you are imprisoned in a character you created for yourself who seemed smart and cheerful and virtuous and now feels like a wooden costume, heavy, clunky. —Perhaps you have been banged around by various events and are a little, how shall we say, *oysgeshpilt*, and need something to make sense. —Perhaps you have sat in a doctor's office listening to his spiel about leakage in the mitral valve and congestive heart disease and suddenly realized *bwannggg* this is *your* mitral valve under discussion and you are headed for a scary ride down the canyon toward surgery. A stranger will shave your private areas and anoint you with antiseptic and slide you onto a gurney and you'll be wheeled into a chilly room with bright overhead lights and a kind lady will begin telling you about anesthesia as one would explain darkness to a small child.

This is a book of poems that if I knew you better and if you were in a hard passage I might send you one or two of along with a note, the way people used to do, believing in the bracing effect of bold writing. Whether you stole the book, bought it used or remaindered, found it on the bus, got it from your son for Christmas, I hope it does you some good. That was the reason for putting the poems together. These poems describe a common life. It is good to know about this. I hope you take courage from it.

I

KINDNESS TO SNAILS

Break of Day

Galway Kinnell

He turns the light on, lights
the cigarette, goes out on the porch,
chainsaws a block of green wood down the grain,
chucks the pieces into the box stove,
pours in kerosene, tosses in the match
he has set fire to the next cigarette with,
stands back while the creosote-lined, sheet-
metal rust-lengths shudder but just barely
manage to direct the *cawhoosh* in the stove—
which sucks in ash motes through gaps
at the bottom and glares out fire blaze
through overburn-cracks at the top—
all the way to the roof and up out through into
the still starry sky starting to lighten,
sits down to a bowl of crackers and bluish milk
in which reflections of a 40-watt ceiling bulb
appear and disappear, eats, contemplates
an atmosphere containing kerosene stink,
chainsaw smoke, chainsmoke, wood smoke, wood heat,
gleams of the 40-watt ceiling bulb bobbing in blue milk.

Happiness

Raymond Carver

So early it's still almost dark out.
I'm near the window with coffee,
and the usual early morning stuff
that passes for thought.
When I see the boy and his friend
walking up the road
to deliver the newspaper.
They wear caps and sweaters,
and one boy has a bag over his shoulder.
They are so happy
they aren't saying anything, these boys.
I think if they could, they would take
each other's arm.
It's early in the morning,
and they are doing this thing together.
They come on, slowly.
The sky is taking on light,
though the moon still hangs pale over the water.
Such beauty that for a minute
death and ambition, even love,
doesn't enter into this.
Happiness. It comes on
unexpectedly. And goes beyond, really,
any early morning talk about it.

This Morning

Jane Kenyon

The barn bears the weight
of the first heavy snow
without complaint.

White breath of cows
rises in the tie-up, a man
wearing a frayed winter jacket
reaches for his milking stool
in the dark.

The cows have gone into the ground,
and the man,
his wife beside him now.

A nuthatch drops
to the ground, feeding
on sunflower seed and bits of bread
I scattered on the snow.

The cats doze near the stove.
They lift their heads
as the plow goes down the road,
making the house
tremble as it passes.

The Monks of St. John's File in for Prayer

Kilian McDonnell

In we shuffle, hooded amplitudes,
scapulared brooms, a stray earring, skin-heads
and flowing locks, blind in one eye,
hooked-nosed, handsome as a prince
(and knows it), a five-thumbed organist,
an acolyte who sings in quarter tones,
one slightly swollen keeper of the bees,
the carpenter minus a finger here and there,
our pre-senile writing deathless verse,
a stranded sailor, a Cassian scholar,
the artist suffering the visually
illiterate and indignities unnamed,
two determined liturgists. In a word,
eager purity and weary virtue.
Last of all, the Lord Abbot, early old
(shepherding the saints is like herding cats).
These chariots and steeds of Israel
make a black progress into church.
A rumble of monks bows low and offers praise
to the High God of Gods who is faithful forever.

Job

(*Job* 28:28)

William Baer

Yes: wisdom begins with *fear* of the Lord,
which comprehends the power that made the seas,
the earth, the shimmering dawn, the unexplored
unfathomed skies, the moon, and the Pleiades.
Which also know Who comes to judge our shoddy
little failing lives, knowing full well,
we need not *fear* the one who kills the body,
but only He who condemns the soul to hell.
Which also knows it magnifies the Lord,
defying the demon, being the only release,
oddly enough, from *fear*, being its own reward,
which is also wise, is faith, is hope, is peace,
is tender mercy, over and over again,
until, at last, is love, is *love*. Amen.

Or Death and December

George Garrett

The Roman Catholic bells of Princeton, New Jersey,
wake me from rousing dreams into a resounding hangover.
Sweet Jesus, my life is hateful to me.
Seven a.m. and time to walk my dog on a leash.

Ice on the sidewalk and in the gutters,
and the wind comes down our one-way street
like a deuce-and-a-half, a six-by, a semi,
huge with a cold load of growls.

There's not one leaf left to bear witness,
with twitch and scuttle, rattle and rasp,
against the blatant roaring of the wrongway wind.
Only my nose running and my face frozen

into a kind of a grin which has nothing to do
with the ice and the wind or death and December,
but joy pure and simple when my black and tan puppy,
for the first time ever, lifts his hind leg to pee.

Sonnet: "Rarely, Rarely Comest Thou, Spirit of Delight"

Gavin Ewart

So you come into the kitchen one morning
(the only room with cat-flap access)
and you find the larger cat, covered in blood, on a chair
and patches of blood on the chair and the floor.
His left foreleg is limp, he can't move it
from the wrist, as it were. A car, a tom-cat?
A dog, or even a suburban fox?
Pathetic, when you stroke him he still gives a very faint purr.

He limps about, on drugs. Two weeks, the damaged nerve is
    healing.
Our Alleluias go up. Because we're there and see it
it's like the end of a famine in Ethiopia—
more real, for us! The genuine rejoicing
that shakes a people at the end of a war—
crowds drinking, singing, splashing in the fountains!

the little horse is newlY

E.E. Cummings

the little horse is newlY

Born)he knows nothing,and feels
everything;all around whom is

perfectly a strange
ness Of sun
light and of fragrance and of

Singing)is ev
erywhere(a welcom
ing dream:is amazing)
a worlD.and in

this world lies:smoothbeautifuL
ly folded;a(brea
thing and a gro

Wing)silence,who;
is:somE

oNe.

A Poem for Emily

Miller Williams

Small fact and fingers and farthest one from me,
a hand's width and two generations away,
in this still present I am fifty-three.
You are not yet a full day.

When I am sixty-three, when you are ten,
and you are neither closer nor as far,
your arms will fill with what you know by then,
the arithmetic and love we do and are.

When I by blood and luck am eighty-six
and you are someplace else and thirty-three
believing in sex and god and politics
with children who look not at all like me,

sometime I know you will have read them this
so they will know I love them and say so
and love their mother. Child, whatever is
is always or never was. Long ago,

a day I watched awhile beside your bed,
I wrote this down, a thing that might be kept
awhile, to tell you what I would have said
when you were who knows what and I was dead
which is I stood and loved you while you slept.

For a Five-Year-Old

Fleur Adcock

A snail is climbing up the window-sill
into your room, after a night of rain.
You call me in to see, and I explain
that it would be unkind to leave it there:
it might crawl to the floor; we must take care
that no one squashes it. You understand,
and carry it outside, with careful hand,
to eat a daffodil.

I see, then, that a kind of faith prevails:
your gentleness is moulded still by words
from me, who have trapped mice and shot wild birds,
from me, who drowned your kittens, who betrayed
your closest relatives, and who purveyed
the harshest kind of truth to many another.
But that is how things are: I am your mother,
and we are kind to snails.

For My Daughter in Reply to a Question

David Ignatow

We're not going to die,
we'll find a way.
We'll breathe deeply
and eat carefully.
We'll think always on life.
There'll be no fading for you or for me.
We'll be the first
and we'll not laugh at ourselves ever
and your children will be my grandchildren.
Nothing will have changed
except by addition.
There'll never be another as you
and never another as I.
No one ever will confuse you
nor confuse me with another.
We will not be forgotten and passed over
and buried under the births and deaths to come.

The Goose

Muriel Spark

Do you want to know why I am alive today?
I will tell you.
Early on, during the food-shortage,
Some of us were miraculously presented
Each with a goose that laid a golden egg.
Myself, I killed the cackling thing and I ate it.
Alas, many and many of the other recipients
Died of gold-dust poisoning.

Starting the Subaru at Five Below

Stuart Kestenbaum

After 6 Maine winters and 100,000 miles,
when I take it to be inspected

I search for gas stations where they
just say beep the horn and don't ask me to

put it on the lift, exposing its soft
rusted underbelly. Inside is the record

of commuting: apple cores, a bag from
McDonald's, crushed Dunkin' Donuts cups,

a flashlight that doesn't work and one
that does, gas receipts blurred beyond

recognition. Finger tips numb, nose
hair frozen, I pump the accelerator

and turn the key. The battery cranks,
the engine gives 2 or 3 low groans and

starts. My God it starts. And unlike
my family in the house, the job I'm

headed towards, the poems in my briefcase,
the dreams I had last night, there is

no question about what makes sense.
White exhaust billowing from the tail pipe,

heater blowing, this car is going to
move me, it's going to take me places.

Day Bath

Debra Spencer

for my son

Last night I walked him back and forth,
his small head heavy against my chest,
round eyes watching me in the dark,
his body a sandbag in my arms.
I longed for sleep but couldn't bear his crying
so bore him back and forth until the sun rose
and he slept. Now the doors are open,
noon sunlight coming in,
and I can see fuchsias opening.
Now we bathe. I hold him, the soap
makes our skins glide past each other.
I lay him wet on my thighs, his head on my knees,
his feet dancing against my chest,
and I rinse him, pouring water
from my cupped hand.
No matter how I feel, he's the same,
eyes expectant, mouth ready,
with his fat legs and arms,
his belly, his small solid back.
Last night I wanted nothing more
than to get him out of my arms.
Today he fits neatly
along the hollow my thighs make,
and with his fragrant skin against mine
I feel brash, like a sunflower.

2

SUCH AS IT IS
MORE OR LESS

A Dialogue of Watching

Kenneth Rexroth

Let me celebrate you. I
Have never known anyone
More beautiful than you. I
Walking beside you, watching
You move beside me, watching
That still grace of hand and thigh,
Watching your face change with words
You do not say, watching your
Solemn eyes as they turn to me,
Or turn inward, full of knowing,
Slow or quick, watching your full
Lips part and smile or turn grave,
Watching your narrow waist, your
Proud buttocks in their grace, like
A sailing swan, an animal,
Free, your own, and never
To be subjugated, but
Abandoned, as I am to you,
Overhearing your perfect
Speech of motion, of love and
Trust and security as
You feed or play with our children.
I have never known any
One more beautiful than you.

A Birthday

W. S. Merwin

Something continues and   I don't know what to call it
though the language is full of suggestions
in the way of language
                              but they are all anonymous
and it's almost your birthday   music next to my bones

these nights we hear the horses   running in the rain
it stops and the moon comes out   and we are still here
the leaks in the roof go on dripping   after the rain has passed
smell of ginger flowers   slips through the dark house
down near the sea   the slow heart of the beacon flashes

the long way to you is still tied to me   but it brought me to you
I keep wanting to give you   what is already yours
it is the morning   of the mornings together
breath of summer   oh my found one
the sleep in the same current   and each waking to you

when I open my eyes   you are what I wanted to see

Thoughts in a Garden

Andrew Marvell

What wondrous life is this I lead!
Ripe apples drop about my head;
The luscious clusters of the vine
Upon my mouth do crush their wine;
The nectarine and curious peach
Into my hands themselves do reach;
Stumbling on melons, as I pass,
Ensnared with flowers, I fall on grass.

Meanwhile the mind from pleasure less
Withdraws into its happiness;
The mind, that Ocean where each kind
Does straight its own resemblance find;
Yet it creates, transcending these,
Far other worlds, and other seas;
Annihilating all that's made
To a green thought in a green shade.

Spring

Mary Oliver

Somewhere
  a black bear
    has just risen from sleep
    and is staring

down the mountain.
  All night
    in the brisk and shallow restlessness
    of early spring

I think of her,
  her four black fists
    flicking the gravel,
    her tongue

like a red fire
  touching the grass,
    the cold water.
      There is only one question:

how to love this world.
  I think of her
    rising
      like a black and leafy ledge

to sharpen her claws against
the silence
of the trees.
Whatever else

my life is
with its poems
and its music
and its glass cities,

it is also this dazzling darkness
coming
down the mountain,
breathing and tasting;

all day I think of her—
her white teeth,
her wordlessness,
her perfect love.

Unharvested

Robert Frost

A scent of ripeness from over a wall.
And come to leave the routine road
And look for what had made me stall,
There sure enough was an apple tree
That had eased itself of its summer load,
And of all but its trivial foliage free,
Now breathed as light as a lady's fan.
For there there had been an apple fall
As complete as the apple had given man.
The ground was one circle of solid red.

May something go always unharvested!
May much stay out of our stated plan,
Apples or something forgotten and left,
So smelling their sweetness would be no theft.

The State of the Economy

Louis Jenkins

There might be some change on top of the dresser at the back, and we should check the washer and the dryer. Check under the floor mats of the car. The couch cushions. I have some books and CDs I could sell, and there are a couple of big bags of aluminum cans in the basement, only trouble is that there isn't enough gas in the car to get around the block. I'm expecting a check sometime next week, which, if we are careful, will get us through to payday. In the meantime with your one-dollar rebate check and a few coins we have enough to walk to the store and buy a quart of milk and a newspaper. On second thought, forget the newspaper.

At the Arraignment

Debra Spencer

The courtroom walls are bare and the prisoner wears
a plastic bracelet, like in a hospital. Jesus stands beside him.
The bailiff hands the prisoner a clipboard and he puts his
thumbprint on the sheet of white paper. The judge asks,

What is your monthly income? *A hundred dollars.*
How do you support yourself? *As a carpenter, odd jobs.*
Where are you living? *My friend's garage.*
What sort of vehicle do you drive? *I take the bus.*
How do you plead? *Not guilty.* The judge sets bail
and a date for the prisoner's trial, calls for the interpreter
so he may speak to the next prisoners.
In a good month I eat, the third one tells him.
In a bad month I break the law.

The judge sighs. The prisoners
are led back to jail with a clink of chains.
Jesus goes with them. More prisoners
are brought before the judge.

Jesus returns and leans against the wall near us,
gazing around the courtroom. The interpreter reads a book.
The bailiff, weighed down by his gun, stands
with arms folded, alert and watchful.
We are only spectators, careful to speak
in low voices. We are so many. If we make a sound,
the bailiff turns toward us, looking stern.

The judge sets bail and dates for other trials,
bringing his gavel down like a little axe.
Jesus turns to us. *If you won't help them,* he says
then do this for me. Dress in silks and jewels,
and then go naked. Be stoic, and then be prodigal.
Lead exemplary lives, then go down into prison
and be bound in chains. Which of us has never broken a law?
I died for you—a desperate extravagance, even for me.
If you can't be merciful, at least be bold.

The judge gets up to leave.

The stern bailiff cries, *All rise.*

from "Song of Myself"

Walt Whitman

The pure contralto sings in the organ loft,
The carpenter dresses his plank, the tongue of his
    foreplane whistles its wild ascending lisp,
The married and unmarried children ride home to their
    Thanksgiving dinner,
The pilot seizes the king-pin, he heaves down with a strong
    arm,
The mate stands braced in the whale-boat, lance and harpoon
    are ready,
The duck-shooter walks by silent and cautious stretches,
The deacons are ordain'd with cross'd hands at the altar,
The lunatic is carried at last to the asylum a confirm'd case,
(He will never sleep any more as he did in the cot in his
    mother's bed-room;)
The jour printer with gray head and gaunt jaws works at
    his case,
He turns his quid of tobacco while his eyes blurr with the
    manuscript;
The malform'd limbs are tied to the surgeon's table,
What is removed drops horribly in a pail;
The quadroon girl is sold at the auction-stand, the drunkard
    nods by the bar-room stove,
The machinist rolls up his sleeves, the policeman
    travels his beat, the gate-keeper marks who pass,

The young fellow drives the express-wagon, (I love him,
    though I do not know him;)
The half-breed straps on his light boots to compete in
    the race,
The bugle calls in the ball-room, the gentlemen run for their
    partners, the dancers bow to each other,
The youth lies awake in the cedar-roof'd garret and harks to
    the musical rain,
The Wolverine sets traps on the creek that helps fill the
    Huron,
The reformer ascends the platform, he spouts with his
    mouth and nose,
The company returns from its excursion, the darkey brings
    up the rear and bears the well-riddled target,
The squaw wrapt in her yellow-hemmed cloth is offering
    moccasins and beadbags for sale,
The connoisseur peers along the exhibition-gallery with
    half-shut eyes bent sideways,
As the deck-hands make fast the steamboat the plank is thrown
    for the shore-going passengers,
The paving-man leans on his two-handed rammer, the
    reporter's lead flies swiftly over the note-book, the
    sign-painter is lettering with blue and gold,
The canal boy trots on the tow-path, the book-keeper counts
    at his desk, the shoemaker waxes his thread,
The conductor beats time for the band and all the performers
    follow him,
The child is baptized, the convert is making the first
    professions,
The regatta is spread on the bay, how the white sails
    sparkle!
The drover watching his drove sings out to them that
    would stray,

The pedler sweats with his pack on his back, (the purchaser
   higgling about the odd cent;)
The bride unrumples her white dress, the minute-hand of the
   clock moves slowly,
The President, holding a cabinet council is surrounded by
   the great Secretaries,
On the piazza walk three matrons stately and friendly with
   twined arms,
The crew of the fish-smack pack repeated layers of halibut in
   the hold,
The Missourian crosses the plains toting his wares and his
   cattle,
As the fare-collector goes through the train he gives notice
   by the jingling of loose change,
The floor-men are laying the floor, the tinners are tinning
   the roof, the masons are calling for mortar,
In single file each shouldering his hod pass onward the
   laborers;
Flatboatmen make fast, towards dusk, near the cotton-wood
   or pecan-trees,
Coon-seekers go through the regions of the Red
   river or through those drain'd by the Tennessee, or
   through those of the Arkansas,
Torches shine in the dark that hangs on the
   Chattahoochee or Altamahaw,
Patriarchs sit at supper with sons and grandsons and great-
   grandsons around them,
In walls of adobie, in canvas tents, rest hunters and trappers
   after their day's sport.
The city sleeps and the country sleeps,
The living sleep for their time, the dead sleep
   for their time,

The old husband sleeps by his wife and the young husband
    sleeps by his wife;
And these tend inward to me, and I tend outward to them,
And such as it is to be of these, more or less, I am,
And of these one and all I weave the song of myself.

Ice Storm

Jane Kenyon

For the hemlocks and broad-leafed evergreens
a beautiful and precarious state of being. . . .
Here in the suburbs of New Haven
nature, unrestrained, lops the weaker limbs
of shrubs and trees with a sense of aesthetics
that is practical and sinister. . . .

I am the guest in this house.
On the bedside table *Good Housekeeping*, and
A Nietzsche Reader. . . . The others are still asleep.
The most painful longing comes over me.
A longing not of the body. . . .

It could be for beauty—
I mean what Keats was panting after,
for which I love and honor him;
it could be for the promises of God;
or for oblivion, *nada*; or some condition even more
extreme, which I intuit, but can't quite name.

Passengers

Billy Collins

At the gate, I sit in a row of blue seats
with the possible company of my death,
this sprawling miscellany of people—
carry-on bags and paperbacks—

that could be gathered in a flash
into a band of pilgrims on the last open road.
Not that I think
if our plane crumpled into a mountain

we would all ascend together,
holding hands like a ring of sky divers,
into a sudden gasp of brightness,
or that there would be some common spot

for us to reunite to jubilize the moment,
some spaceless, pillarless Greece
where we could, at the count of three,
toss our ashes into the sunny air.

It's just that the way that man has his briefcase
so carefully arranged,
the way that girl is cooling her tea,
and the flow of the comb that woman

passes through her daughter's hair . . .
and when you consider the altitude,
the secret parts of the engines,
and all the hard water and the deep canyons below . . .

well, I just think it would be good if one of us
maybe stood up and said a few words,
or, so as not to involve the police,
at least quietly wrote something down.

The Summer-Camp Bus
Pulls Away from the Curb

Sharon Olds

Whatever he needs, he has or doesn't
have by now.
Whatever the world is going to do to him
it has started to do. With a pencil and two
Hardy Boys and a peanut butter sandwich and
grapes he is on his way, there is nothing
more we can do for him. Whatever is
stored in his heart, he can use, now.
Whatever he has laid up in his mind
he can call on. What he does not have
he can lack. The bus gets smaller and smaller, as one
folds a flag at the end of a ceremony,
onto itself, and onto itself, until
only a heavy wedge remains.
Whatever his exuberant soul
can do for him, it is doing right now.
Whatever his arrogance can do
it is doing to him. Everything
that's been done to him, he will now do.
Everything that's been placed in him
will come out, now, the contents of a trunk
unpacked and lined up on a bunk in the underpine light.

you can take it with you

Josephine Jacobsen

2 little girls who live next door
to this house are on their trampoline.
the window is closed, so they are soundless.

the sun slants, it is going away:
but now it hits full on the trampoline
and the small figure on each end.

alternately they fly up to the sun,
fly, and rebound, fly, are shot
up, fly, are shot up up.

one comes down in the lotus
position. the other, outdone,
somersaults in air. their hair

flies too. nothing, nothing, noth
ing can keep them down. the air
sucks them up by the hair of their heads.

i know all about what is
happening in this city at just
this moment, every last

grain of dark, i conceive.
but what i see now is
the 2 little girls flung up

flung up, the sun snatch
ing them, their mouths rounded
in gasps. they are there, they fly up.

SUCH AS IT IS MORE OR LESS · 39

To David, About His Education

Howard Nemerov

The world is full of mostly invisible things,
And there is no way but putting the mind's eye,
Or its nose, in a book, to find them out,
Things like the square root of Everest
Or how many times Byron goes into Texas,
Or whether the law of the excluded middle
Applies west of the Rockies. For these
And the like reasons, you have to go to school
And study books and listen to what you are told,
And sometimes try to remember. Though I don't know
What you will do with the mean annual rainfall
On Plato's Republic, or the calorie content
Of the Diet of Worms, such things are said to be
Good for you, and you will have to learn them
In order to become one of the grown-ups
Who sees invisible things neither steadily nor whole,
But keeps gravely the grand confusion of the world
Under his hat, which is where it belongs,
And teaches small children to do this in their turn.

Invitation

Carl Dennis

This is your invitation to the Ninth-Grade Play
At Jackson Park Middle School
8:00 P.M., November 17, 1947.
Macbeth, authored by Shakespeare
And directed by Mr. Grossman and Mrs. Silvio
With scenery from Miss Ferguson's art class.

A lot of effort has gone into it.
Dozens of students have chosen to stay after school
Week after week with their teachers
Just to prepare for this one evening,
A gift to lift you a moment beyond the usual.
Even if you've moved away, you'll want to return.
Jackson Park, in case you've forgotten, stands
At the end of Jackson Street at the top of the hill.

Doubtless you recall that *Macbeth* is about ambition.
This is the play for you if you've been tempted
To claw your way to the top. If you haven't been,
It should make you feel grateful.
Just allow time to get lost before arriving.
So many roads are ready to take you forward
Into the empty world to come, misty with promises.
So few will lead you back to what you've missed.

Just get an early start.
Call in sick to the office this once.
Postpone your vacation a day or two.
Prepare to find the road neglected,
The street signs rusted, the school dark,
The doors locked, the windows broken.
This is where the challenge comes in.

Do you suppose our country would have been settled
If the pioneers had worried about being lonely?

Somewhere the students are speaking the lines
You can't remember. Somewhere, days before that,
This invitation went out, this one you're reading
On your knees in the attic, the contents of a trunk
Piled beside you. Forget about your passport.
You don't need to go to Paris just yet.
Europe will seem even more beautiful
Once you complete the journey you begin today.

Calling him back from layoff

Bob Hicok

I called a man today. After he said
hello and I said hello came a pause
during which it would have been

confusing to say hello again so I said
how are you doing and guess what, he said
fine and wondered aloud how I was

and it turns out I'm OK. He
was on the couch watching cars
painted with ads for Budweiser follow cars

painted with ads for Tide around an oval
that's a metaphor for life because
most of us run out of gas and settle

for getting drunk in the stands
and shouting at someone in a t-shirt
we want kraut on our dog. I said

he could have his job back and during
the pause that followed his whiskers
scrubbed the mouthpiece clean

and his breath passed in and out
in the tidal fashion popular
with mammals until he broke through

with the words *how soon thank you*
ohmyGod which crossed his lips and drove
through the wires on the backs of ions

as one long word as one hard prayer
of relief meant to be heard
by the sky. When he began to cry I tried

with the shape of my silence to say
I understood but each confession
of fear and poverty was more awkward

than what you learn in the shower.
After he hung up I went outside and sat
with one hand in the bower of the other

and thought if I turn my head to the left
it changes the song of the oriole
and if I give a job to one stomach other

forks are naked and if tonight a steak
sizzles in his kitchen do the seven
other people staring at their phones

hear?

Working in the Rain

Robert Morgan

My father loved more than anything to
work outside in wet weather. Beginning
at daylight he'd go out in dripping brush
to mow or pull weeds for hog and chickens.
First his shoulders got damp and the drops from
his hat ran down his back. When even his
armpits were soaked he came in to dry out
by the fire, make coffee, read a little.
But if the rain continued he'd soon be
restless, and go out to sharpen tools in
the shed or carry wood in from the pile,
then open up a puddle to the drain,
working by steps back into the downpour.
I thought he sought the privacy of rain,
the one time no one was likely to be
out and he was left to the intimacy
of drops touching every leaf and tree in
the woods and the easy muttering of
drip and runoff, the shine of pools behind
grass dams. He could not resist the long
ritual, the companionship and freedom
of falling weather, or even the cold
drenching, the heavy soak and chill of clothes
and sobbing of fingers and sacrifice
of shoes that earned a baking by the fire
and washed fatigue after the wandering
and loneliness in the country of rain.

My Father's Lunch

Erica Funkhouser

Saturday afternoon,
he'd sit at the kitchen table
in khakis and a workshirt.
White napkin, a beer, the serrated knife.
Pieces of prosciutto or headcheese
or kippered herring
layered on slabs of black bread.

Outside, the ripe hayfields
or the stacks of shutters
or the forest needing to be cleared
or the snow needing to be pushed aside
lay still as they waited for him
to finish his lunch.

For now he was ours,
whether he smelled of chokecherry,
tractor oil, or twine.
He'd washed his hands
with brown naphtha soap
and splashed water onto his face
and shaken it off like a dog.
He'd offer more ham, more bread
to anyone who sat down.

This was work, too,
but he did it slowly, with no impatience,
not yet reminding the older boys
that he'd need them later
or asking the smaller children
if we'd stored the apples
or shoved last year's hay
out of the wonderful window
to nowhere.

This was the interlude
of nearly translucent slices,
of leaning back in the smooth wooden chair
and wiping white foam from his lip
as the last beads of beer rose calmly
to the surface of the glass.
We could see it was an old meal
with the patina of dream
going back to the first days
of bread and meat and work.

All our lives, my brothers,
my sister, and I will eat
this same meal, savoring
its provisional peace,
like the peace in the grain room
after we'd scooped the grain
from the bins, and the sticky oats
and the agitated flakes of bran
had slipped back down into the soft valleys
where they would remain
until it was time to feed the animals again.

3

THIS LUST OF TENDERNESS

The Happiest Day

Linda Pastan

It was early May, I think
a moment of lilac or dogwood
when so many promises are made
it hardly matters if a few are broken.
My mother and father still hovered
in the background, part of the scenery
like the houses I had grown up in,
and if they would be torn down later
that was something I knew
but didn't believe. Our children were asleep
or playing, the youngest as new
as the new smell of the lilacs,
and how could I have guessed
their roots were shallow
and would be easily transplanted.
I didn't even guess that I was happy.
The small irritations that are like salt
on melon were what I dwelt on,
though in truth they simply
made the fruit taste sweeter.
So we sat on the porch
in the cool morning, sipping
hot coffee. Behind the news of the day—
strikes and small wars, a fire somewhere—
I could see the top of your dark head
and thought not of public conflagrations

but of how it would feel on my bare shoulder.
If someone could stop the camera then . . .
if someone could only stop the camera
and ask me: are you happy?
perhaps I would have noticed
how the morning shone in the reflected
color of lilac. Yes, I might have said
and offered a steaming cup of coffee.

'After dark vapours have oppressed our plains'

John Keats

After dark vapours have oppressed our plains
   For a long dreary season, comes a day
   Born of the gentle South, and clears away
From the sick heavens all unseemly stains.
The anxious month, relieving from its pains,
   Takes as a long-lost right the feel of May,
   The eyelids with the passing coolness play,
Like rose leaves with the drip of summer rains.
And calmest thoughts come round us—as of leaves
   Budding—fruit ripening in stillness—autumn suns
Smiling at eve upon the quiet sheaves—
Sweet Sappho's cheek—a sleeping infant's breath—
   The gradual sand through an hour-glass runs—
A woodland rivulet—a Poet's death.

Children's Hospital, Emergency Room

Gregory Djanikian

You do not want to be here
You wish it were you
The doctor is stitching up
It is a cut on the chin, fixable
This time but deep enough
To make you think of gashes
Puncture wounds flesh unfolding to the bone
Your child is lying on the table
Restrained, You must be still
The nurse who cradles her head is saying
And the doctor is embroidering
Delicately patiently like a kind aunt
But there is not enough solace in that
To make you stop thinking of other children
Whose hurt blooms like a dark interior bruise
In other rooms there is hysteria
The sound of glass shattering
And in the next bay there is the child
Who is sleeping too soundly
You do not want to hear such silence
The evidence which convicts, puts away
Wake up, you whisper, wake up
You want to think of water
A surface with no scars
You want the perpetuity of circles
A horizon clear and unbroken

And the sky a flat blue immensity
Without sides or depth
But there is nothing you can do
When your daughter calls out It hurts
And things regain their angularity
The vulnerable opaqueness, I'm here
You say, Be still, I'm here
Though you wish none of you were
And if anyone offered you now the life
Of the spirit you would take it for all of you
The child asleep or your child
Those in pain or mercifully out
You would take it and fly though never
Would you feel this rush of joy
As you do now when your daughter
Is returned to you unhealed but whole
Your lips pressing against her cheek
And your hands hovering
Like two shy birds about her face.

The Longly-Weds Know

Leah Furnas

That it isn't about the Golden Anniversary at all,
But about all the unremarkable years
that Hallmark doesn't even make a card for.

It's about the 2nd anniversary when they were surprised
to find they cared for each other more than last year

And the 4th when both kids had chickenpox
and she threw her shoe at him for no real reason

And the 6th when he accidentally got drunk on the way
home from work because being a husband and father
was so damn hard

It's about the 11th and 12th and 13th years when
they discovered they could survive crisis

And the 22nd anniversary when they looked
at each other across the empty nest, and found it good.

It's about the 37th year when she finally
decided she could never change him

And the 38th when he decided
a little change wasn't that bad

It's about the 46th anniversary when they both
bought cards, and forgot to give them to each other

But most of all it's about the end of the 49th year
when they discovered you don't have to be old

to have your 50th anniversary!!!!

In Answer to Your Query

Naomi Lazard

We are sorry to inform you
the item you ordered
is no longer being produced.
It has not gone out of style
nor have people lost interest in it.
In fact, it has become
one of our most desired products.
Its popularity is still growing.
Orders for it come in
at an ever increasing rate.
However, a top-level decision
has caused this product
to be discontinued forever.

Instead of the item you ordered
we are sending you something else.
It is not the same thing,
nor is it a reasonable facsimile.
It is what we have in stock,
the very best we can offer.

If you are not happy
with this substitution
let us know as soon as possible.
As you can imagine

we already have quite an accumulation
of letters such as the one
you may or may not write.
To be totally fair
We respond to these complaints
as they come in.
Yours will be filed accordingly,
answered in its turn.

Toast

Leonard Nathan

There was a woman in Ithaca
who cried softly all night
in the next room and helpless
I fell in love with her under the blanket
of snow that settled on all the roofs
of the town, filling up
every dark depression.

Next morning
in the motel coffee shop
I studied all the made-up faces
of women. Was it the middle-aged blonde
who kidded the waitress
or the young brunette lifting
her cup like a toast?

Love, whoever you are,
your courage was my companion
for many cold towns
after the betrayal of Ithaca,
and when I order coffee
in a strange place, still
I say, lifting, this is for you.

Detail Waiting for a Train

Stanley Plumly

The main floor of Penn Station, early,
the first commuters arriving, leaving,
the man outstretched on his coat,
wide circles of survivors forming.

He's half in, half out of his clothes,
being kissed and cardio-shocked,
though he was likely dead before he landed.

This goes on for minutes, minutes more,
until the medics unhook the vanished heart,
move him onto the cot and cover him
with the snow-depth of a sheet

and wheel him the fluorescent length
of the hall through gray freight doors
that open on their own and close at will.

September Twelfth, 2001

X. J. Kennedy

Two caught on film who hurtle
from the eighty-second floor,
choosing between a fireball
and to jump holding hands,

aren't us. I wake beside you,
stretch, scratch, taste the air,
the incredible joy of coffee
and the morning light.

Alive, we open eyelids
on our pitiful share of time,
we bubbles rising and bursting
in a boiling pot.

The Altar

Charles Simic

The plastic statue of the Virgin
On top of a bedroom dresser
With a blackened mirror
From a bad-dream grooming salon.

Two pebbles from the grave of a rock star,
A small, grinning windup monkey,
A bronze Egyptian coin
And a red movie-ticket stub.

A splotch of sunlight on the framed
Communion photograph of a boy
With the eyes of someone
Who will drown in a lake real soon.

An altar dignifying the god of chance.
What is beautiful, it cautions,
Is found accidentally and not sought after.
What is beautiful is easily lost.

Sonnet No. 6: Dearest,
I never knew such loving

Hayden Carruth

Dearest, I never knew such loving. There
in that glass tower in the alien city, alone,
we found what somewhere I had always known
exists and must exist, this fervent care,
this lust of tenderness. Two were aware
how in hot seizure, bone pressed to bone
and liquid flesh to flesh, each separate moan
was pleasure, yes, but most in each other's share.
Companions and discoverers, equal and free,
so deep in love we adventured and so far
that we became perhaps more than we are,
and now being home is hardship. Therefore are we
diminished? No. We are of the world again
but still augmented, more than we've ever been.

There Comes the Strangest Moment

Kate Light

There comes the strangest moment in your life,
when everything you thought before breaks free—
what you relied upon, as ground-rule and as rite
looks upside down from how it used to be.

Skin's gone pale, your brain is shedding cells;
you question every tenet you set down;
obedient thoughts have turned to infidels
and every verb desires to be a noun.

I want—my want. I love—my love. I'll stay
with you. I thought transitions were the best,
but I want what's here to never go away.
I'll make my peace, my bed, and kiss this breast . . .

Your heart's in retrograde. You simply have no choice.
Things people told you turn out to be true.
You have to hold that body, hear that voice.
You'd have sworn no one knew you more than you.

How many people thought you'd never change?
But here you have. It's beautiful. It's strange.

Snowflake

William Baer

Timing's everything. The vapor rises
high in the sky, tossing to and fro,
then freezes, suddenly, and crystalizes
into a perfect flake of miraculous snow.
For countless miles, drifting east above
the world, whirling about in a swirling free-
for-all, appearing aimless, just like love,
but sensing, seeking out, its destiny.
Falling to where the two young skaters stand,
hand in hand, then flips and dips and whips
itself about to ever-so-gently land,
a miracle, across her unkissed lips:
as he blocks the wind raging from the south,
leaning forward to kiss her lovely mouth.

Somewhere I'll Find You

Phebe Hanson

So we moved from my small town in western Minnesota
to St. Paul where I had to go to Murray High, a school
with more people than in the entire town of Sacred Heart,

and I had to walk two and a half miles every day because
there were no school buses, but it turned out to be not so
bad after all because I met a boy in confirmation class who

let me ride on the handlebars of his bike on the way home from
school and one Sunday my dad even let this boy pick me up
to go for a walk in Como Park, since after all the paths were

safe, filled with many families swarming with children, and
even though my dad knew the devil went about the city like a
roaring lion seeking whom he might devour, he let me go

with this boy because after all he was a Luther Leaguer and
we had sung together sitting side by side in church, "Yield not to
temptation, for yielding is sin / each vict'ry will help you,

some other to win / fight manfully onward, dark passions subdue /
look only to Jesus, He'll carry you through," but as soon as we
left my house this boy said he was going to take me some other

place I'd like very much and it was going to be a surprise so
off we went on the streetcar and new to the city I had no idea
        where
we were going until we got off and were standing in front of a

movie marquee and I said, "I can't go in. You know my father
doesn't let me go to movies. It's a sin," but he gently guided me
with his seductive hands, saying "Just come into the lobby to
        talk."

There below the sign "Somewhere I'll Find You," starring Clark
        Gable
and Lana Turner in a "torrid tale of love between two people
        caught
in the chaos of war," he persuaded me at least to go inside and sit

down and watch part of the movie and if I didn't like it, we could
        get
right back on the streetcar and go to Como Park, so I decided
        since
I already was in this lobby den of iniquity surrounded by posters of
Jezebel movie queens and devilish leading men, I was doomed
        anyway,
so I might as well go into the darkness with him and even let him
        put
his arm around me and hold my hand and that's the way it's been
        ever since.

Feasting

Elizabeth W. Garber

I am so amazed to find myself kissing you
with such abandon,
filling myself with our kisses
astounding hunger for edges of lips and tongue.
Returning to feast again and again,
our bellies never overfilling from this banquet.
Returning in surprise,
in remembering,
in rediscovering,
such play of flavors of gliding lips
and forests of pressures and spaces.
The spaces between the branches
as delicious as finding the grove of lilies of the valley
blossoming just outside my door under the ancient oak.
"I've never held anyone this long," you said,
the second time you entered my kitchen.
I am the feast this kitchen was blessed to prepare
waiting for you to enter open mouthed in awe
in the mystery we've been given,
our holy feast.

Song

W. H. Auden

The chimney sweepers
Wash their faces and forget to wash the neck;
The lighthouse keepers
Let the lamps go out and leave the ships to wreck;
The prosperous baker
Leaves the rolls in hundreds in the oven to burn;
The undertaker
Pins a small note on the coffin saying "Wait till I return,
I've got a date with Love."

And deep-sea divers
Cut their boots off and come bubbling to the top,
And engine-drivers
Bring expresses in the tunnel to a stop;
The village rector
Dashes down the side-aisle half-way through a psalm;
The sanitary inspector
Runs off with the cover of the cesspool on his arm—
To keep his date with Love.

Yes

Catherine Doty

It's about the blood
banging in the body,
and the brain
lolling in its bed
like a happy baby.
At your touch, the nerve,
that volatile spook tree,
vibrates. The lungs
take up their work
with a giddy vigor.
Tremors in the joints
and tympani,
dust storms
in the canister of sugar.
The coil of ribs
heats up, begins
to glow. Come
here.

The Dalliance of the Eagles

Walt Whitman

Skirting the river road, (my forenoon walk, my rest,)
Skyward in air a sudden muffled sound, the dalliance of
    the eagles,
The rushing amorous contact high in space together,
The clinching interlocking claws, a living, fierce,
    gyrating wheel,
Four beating wings, two beaks, a swirling mass tight
    grappling,
In tumbling turning clustering loops, straight
    downward falling,
Till o'er the river pois'd, the twain yet one, a moment's
    lull,
A motionless still balance in the air, then parting,
    talons loosing,
Upward again on slow-firm pinions slanting, their
    separate diverse flight,
She hers, he his, pursuing.

After Love

Maxine Kumin

Afterward, the compromise.
Bodies resume their boundaries.

These legs, for instance, mine.
Your arms take you back in.

Spoons of our fingers, lips
admit their ownership.

The bedding yawns, a door
blows aimlessly ajar

and overhead, a plane
singsongs coming down.

Nothing is changed, except
there was a moment when

the wolf, the mongering wolf
who stands outside the self

lay lightly down, and slept.

Sonnet CVI: When in the chronicle of wasted time

William Shakespeare

When in the chronicle of wasted time
I see descriptions of the fairest wights,
And beauty making beautiful old rhyme
In praise of ladies dead and lovely knights,
Then, in the blazon of sweet beauty's best,
Of hand, of foot, of lip, of eye, of brow,
I see their antique pen would have express'd
Even such a beauty as you master now.
So all their praises are but prophecies
Of this our time, all you prefiguring;
And, for they look'd but with divining eyes,
They had not skill enough your worth to sing:
　　For we, which now behold these present days,
　　Had eyes to wonder, but lack tongues to praise.

4

DELIBERATE
OBFUSCATION

A Spiral Notebook

Ted Kooser

The bright wire rolls like a porpoise
in and out of the calm blue sea
of the cover, or perhaps like a sleeper
twisting in and out of his dreams,
for it could hold a record of dreams
if you wanted to buy it for that,
though it seems to be meant for
more serious work, with its
college-ruled lines and its cover
that states in emphatic white letters,
5 SUBJECT NOTEBOOK. It seems
a part of growing old is no longer
to have five subjects, each
demanding an equal share of attention,
set apart by brown cardboard dividers,
but instead to stand in a drugstore
and hang on to one subject
a little too long, like this notebook
you weigh in your hands, passing
your fingers over its surfaces
as if it were some kind of wonder.

What's in My Journal

William Stafford

Odd things, like a button drawer. Mean
things, fishhooks, barbs in your hand.
But marbles too. A genius for being agreeable.
Junkyard crucifixes, voluptuous
discards. Space for knickknacks, and for
Alaska. Evidence to hang me, or to beatify.
Clues that lead nowhere, that never connected
anyway. Deliberate obfuscation, the kind
that takes genius. Chasms in character.
Loud omissions. Mornings that yawn above
a new grave. Pages you know exist
but you can't find them. Someone's terribly
inevitable life story, maybe mine.

Why I Take Good Care of my Macintosh

Gary Snyder

Because it broods under its hood like a perched falcon,
Because it jumps like a skittish horse
    and sometimes throws me
Because it is poky when cold
Because plastic is a sad, strong material
    that is charming to rodents
Because it is flighty
Because my mind flies into it through my fingers
Because it leaps forward and backward,
    is an endless sniffer and searcher,
Because its keys click like hail on a boulder
And it winks when it goes out,

And puts word-heaps in hoards for me,
    dozens of pockets of
    gold under boulders in streambeds, identical seedpods
    strong on a vine, or it stores bins of bolts;
And I lose them and find them,

Because whole worlds of writing can be boldly layed out
    and then highlighted   and vanish in a flash
    at "delete"   so it teaches
    of impermanence and pain;
And because my computer and me are both brief
    in this world, both foolish, and we have earthly fates,
Because I have let it move in with me
    right inside the tent
And it goes with me out every morning
We fill up our baskets,   get back home,
Feel rich,   relax,   I throw it a scrap and it hums.

Ode to My 1977 Toyota

Barbara Hamby

Engine like a Singer sewing machine, where have you
    not carried me—to dance class, grocery shopping,
into the heart of darkness and back again? O the fruit
    you've transported—cherries, peaches, blueberries,
watermelons, thousands of Fuji apples—books,
    and all my dark thoughts, the giddy ones, too,
like bottles of champagne popped at the wedding of two people
    who will pass each other on the street as strangers
in twenty years. Ronald Reagan was president when I walked
    into Big Chief Motors and saw you glimmering
on the lot like a slice of broiled mahi mahi or sushi
    without its topknot of tuna. Remember the months
I drove you to work singing "Some Enchanted Evening"?
    Those were scary times. All I thought about
was getting on I-10 with you and not stopping. Would you
    have made it to New Orleans? What would our life
have been like there? I'd forgotten about poetry. Thank God,
    I remembered her. She saved us both. We were young
together. Now we're not. College boys stop us at traffic lights
    and tell me how cool you are. Like an ice cube, I say,
though you've never had air conditioning. Who needed it?
    I would have missed so many smells without you—
confederate jasmine, magnolia blossoms, the briny sigh
    of the Gulf of Mexico, rotting 'possums scattered
along 319 between Sopchoppy and Panacea. How many holes
    are there in the ballet shoes in your back seat?

How did that pair of men's white loafers end up in your trunk?
    Why do I have so many questions, and why
are the answers like the animals that dart in front of your headlights
    as we drive home from the coast, the Milky Way
strung across the black velvet bowl of the sky like the tiara
    of some impossibly fat empress who rules the universe
but doesn't know if tomorrow is December or Tuesday or June first.

Internal Exile

Richard Cecil

Although most people I know were condemned
years ago by Judge Necessity
to life in condos near a freeway exit
convenient to their twice-a-day commutes
through traffic jams to jobs that they dislike,
they didn't bury their heads in their hands
and cry "Oh, no!" when sentence was pronounced:
Forty years accounting in Duluth!
or *Tenure at Southwest Missouri State!*
    Instead, they mumbled, *not bad. It could be worse,*
when the bailiff, Fate, led them away
to Personnel to fill out payroll forms
and have their smiling ID photos snapped.
And that's what they still mumble every morning
just before their snooze alarms go off
when Fluffy nuzzles them out of their dreams
of making out with movie stars on beaches.
They rise at five a.m. and feed their cats
and drive to work and work and drive back home
and feed their cats and eat and fall asleep
while watching Evening News's fresh disasters—
blown-up bodies littering a desert
fought over for the last three thousand years,
and smashed-to-pieces million-dollar houses
built on islands swept by hurricanes.
It's soothing to watch news about the places

where people literally will die to live
when you live someplace with no attractions—
mountains, coastline, history—like here,
where none aspire to live, though many do.
"A great place to work, with no distractions"
is how my interviewer first described it
nineteen years ago, when he hired me.
And, though he moved the day that he retired
to his dream house in the uplands with a vista,
he wasn't lying—working's better here
and easier than trying to have fun.
Is that the way it is where you're stuck, too?

Burma-Shave

Traditional

THE QUEEN
OF HEARTS
NOW LOVES THE KNAVE
THE KING
RAN OUT OF
BURMA-SHAVE

IF HARMONY
IS WHAT YOU CRAVE
THEN GET
A TUBA
BURMA-SHAVE

IF HONEY SHUNS
YOUR FOND EMBRACE
DON'T SHOOT
THE MILKMAN
FEEL YOUR FACE
BURMA-SHAVE

SLOWDOWN, PA
SAKES ALIVE
MA MISSED SIGNS
FOUR AND FIVE
BURMA-SHAVE

A NUT AT THE WHEEL
A PEACH ON HIS RIGHT
CURVE AHEAD
SALAD TONIGHT
BURMA-SHAVE

IS HE LONESOME
OR JUST BLIND
THAT GUY WHO DRIVES
SO CLOSE BEHIND?
BURMA-SHAVE

IF YOU DRIVE
WHEN YOU'RE DRUNK
CARRY A COFFIN
IN YOUR TRUNK
BURMA-SHAVE

HER CHARIOT RACED
AT EIGHTY PER
THEY HAULED AWAY
WHAT HAD BEN HUR
BURMA-SHAVE

IT GAVE
MCDONALD
THAT NEEDED CHARM
HELLO HOLLYWOOD
GOOD-BYE FARM
BURMA-SHAVE

NO LADY LIKES
TO DANCE
OR DINE
ACCOMPANIED BY
A PORCUPINE
BURMA-SHAVE

THE WHALE TOOK JONAH
DOWN THE HATCH
THEN COUGHED HIM UP
BECAUSE HE SCRATCHED
BURMA-SHAVE

POOR SATAN HE
WAS FORCED
TO DWELL
IN THE ONLY PLACE WHERE
THEY DON'T SELL
BURMA-SHAVE

SCHOOL AHEAD
TAKE IT SLOW
LET THE LITTLE
SHAVERS GROW
BURMA-SHAVE

DOES YOUR HUSBAND MISBEHAVE
GRUNT AND GRUMBLE
RANT AND RAVE?
SHOOT THE BRUTE SOME
BURMA-SHAVE

Carnation Milk

Anonymous

Carnation Milk is the best in the land,
Here I sit with a can in my hand—
No tits to pull, no hay to pitch,
You just punch a hole in the son of a bitch.

A Brief Lecture on Door Closers

Clemens Starck

Although heretofore unconsidered
in verse or in song,
the ordinary door closer is, I submit, a device
well worth considering.
Consisting primarily
of a spring and a piston, in combination,
here's how it works:
　　　　You open a door,
either pushing or pulling.
The spring is compressed, the piston extended.
Now, having passed through the doorway,
you relinquish control,
and the door closer takes over. The spring remembers
how it was—
it wants to return. But the urge is damped
by the resistance the piston encounters,
snug in its cylinder
filled with hydraulic fluid.

Such is the mechanism of the door closer,
invented in 1876
by Charles Norton, when a slamming door
in a courtroom in Cincinnati
repeatedly disrupted
the administration of justice.

Whether concealed beneath the threshold
or overhead in the head jamb,
whether surface-mounted as a parallel-arm installation
or as a regular-arm,
door closers are ever vigilant,
silently performing their function, rarely
complaining.

Whereas doors can be metaphorical—as in,
for example, "He could never unlock
the door to her heart"—
door closers cannot.

Remember this when you
pass through, and the door closes behind you
with a soft thud
and final click
as the latchbolt engages the strike.

Sonnet XII: Why are we by all creatures waited on?

John Donne

Why are we by all creatures waited on?
Why do the prodigal elements supply
Life and food to me, being more pure than I,
Simple, and further from corruption?
Why brook'st thou, ignorant horse, subjection?
Why dost thou bull, and boar so sillily
Dissemble weakness, and by'one man's stroke die,
Whose whole kind you might swallow and feed upon?
Weaker I am, woe is me, and worse than you,
You have not sinned, nor need be timorous.
But wonder at a greater wonder, for to us
Created nature doth these things subdue,
But their Creator, whom sin, nor nature tied,
For us, his creatures, and his foes, hath died.

Angels

Maurya Simon

Who are without mercy,
Who confide in trumpet flowers,
Who carry loose change in their pockets,
Who dress in black velvet,
Who wince and fidget like bats,
Who balance their haloes on hatracks,
Who watch reruns of famine,
Who powder their noses with pollen,
Who laugh and unleash earthquakes,
Who sidle in and out of our dreams
Like magicians, like childhood friends,
Who practice their smiles like pirates,
Who exercise by walking to Zion,
Who live on the edge of doubt,
Who cause vertigo but ease migraines,
Who weep milky tears when troubled,
Whose night sweats engender the plague,
Who pinion their arms to chandeliers,
Who speak in riddles and slant rhymes,
Who love the weak and foolhardy,
Who lust for unripe persimmons,
Who scavenge the fields for lost souls,
Who hover near lighthouses,
Who pray at railroad crossings,
Who supervise the study of rainbows,
Who cannot blush but try,

Who curl their hair with corkscrews,
Who honeymoon with Orion,
Who are not wise but pure,
Who behave with impious propriety,
Who hourly scour our faces with hope,
Whose own faces glow like radium,
Whom we've created in our own form,
Who are without mercy, seek and yearn
To return us like fossilized roses
To the wholeness of our original bloom.

Passing Through a Small Town

David Shumate

Here the highways cross. One heads north. One heads east
and west. On the corner of the square adjacent to the
courthouse a bronze plaque marks the place where two Civil
War generals faced one another and the weaker surrendered.
A few pedestrians pass. A beauty parlor sign blinks. As I turn
to head west, I become the schoolteacher living above the
barber shop. Polishing my shoes each evening. Gazing at the
square below. In time I befriend the waitress at the cafe and
she winks as she pours my coffee. Soon people begin to
talk. And for good reason. I become so distracted I teach my
students that Cleopatra lost her head during the French
Revolution and that Leonardo perfected the railroad at the
height of the Renaissance. One day her former lover returns
from the army and creates a scene at the school. That evening
she confesses she cannot decide between us. But still we spend
one last night together. By the time I pass the grain elevators
on the edge of town I am myself again. The deep scars of love
already beginning to heal.

In Paris with You

James Fenton

Don't talk to me of love. I've had an earful
And I get tearful when I've downed a drink or two.
I'm one of your talking wounded.
I'm a hostage. I'm maroonded.
But I'm in Paris with you.

Yes I'm angry at the way I've been bamboozled
And resentful at the mess that I've been through.
I admit I'm on the rebound
And I don't care where are *we* bound.
I'm in Paris with you.

Do you mind if we do *not* go to the Louvre,
If we say sod off to sodding Notre Dame,
If we skip the Champs Elysées
And remain here in this sleazy
Old hotel room
Doing this and that
To what and whom
Learning who you are,
Learning what I am.

Don't talk to me of love. Let's talk of Paris,
The little bit of Paris in our view.
There's that crack across the ceiling

And the hotel walls are peeling
And I'm in Paris with you.

Don't talk to me of love. Let's talk of Paris.
I'm in Paris with the slightest thing you do.
I'm in Paris with your eyes, your mouth,
I'm in Paris with . . . all points south.
Am I embarrassing you?
I'm in Paris with you.

Wedding Poem
For Schele and Phil

Bill Holm

A marriage is risky business these days
Says some old and prudent voice inside.
We don't need twenty children anymore
To keep the family line alive,
Or gather up the hay before the rain.
No law demands respectability.
Love can arrive without certificate or cash.
History and experience both make clear
That men and women do not hear
The music of the world in the same key,
Rather rolling dissonances doomed to clash.

So what is left to justify a marriage?
Maybe only the hunch that half the world
Will ever be present in any room
With just a single pair of eyes to see it.
Whatever is invisible to one
Is to the other an enormous golden lion
Calm and sleeping in the easy chair.
After many years, if things go right
Both lion and emptiness are always there;
The one never true without the other.

But the dark secret of the ones long married,
A pleasure never mentioned to the young,
Is the sweet heat made from two bodies in a bed
Curled together on a winter night,
The smell of the other always in the quilt,
The hand set quietly on the other's flank
That carries news from another world
Light-years away from the one inside
That you always thought you inhabited alone.
The heat in that hand could melt a stone.

5

THE SOUND OF A CAR

Seven Deadly Sins

Virginia Hamilton Adair

Behold the systematic GLUTTON
who eats the fat first off his mutton,
and while the blessing says, "We're grateful,"
he's asking for a second plateful.

This man is also AVARICIOUS,
finding the smell of dough delicious,
and takes a fierce, uxorious PRIDE
in one possession: his young bride.

His neighbor just across the fence,
a man of strong CONCUPISCENCE,
ENVYING the husband his fair flower,
would buy her favors by the hour.

ANGER inflames the husband's face,
but AVARICE takes the higher place.
He says, "Don't let my ANGER trouble you;
Take her—I'll take your BMW."

The deal is struck; with one car more,
a final sin completes his score.
The sinner says, "I'd shoot them both,
were I not such a slave to SLOTH."

Teaching a Child the Art of Confession

David Shumate

It is best not to begin with Adam and Eve. Original Sin is baffling, even for the most sophisticated minds. Besides, children are frightened of naked people and apples. Instead, start with the talking snake. Children like to hear what animals have to say. Let him hiss for a while and tell his own tale. They'll figure him out in the end. Describe sin simply as those acts which cause suffering and leave it at that. Steer clear of musty confessionals. Children associate them with outhouses. Leave Hell out of the discussion. They'll be able to describe it on their own soon enough. If they feel the need to apologize for some transgression, tell them that one of the offices of the moon is to forgive. As for the priest, let him slumber a while more.

A Physics

Heather McHugh

When you get down to it, Earth
has our own great ranges
of feeling—Rocky, Smoky, Blue—
and a heart that can melt stones.

The still pools fill with sky,
as if aloof, and we have eyes
for all of this—and more, for Earth's
reminding moon. We too are ruled

by such attractions—spun and swaddled,
rocked and lent a light. We run
our clocks on wheels, our trains
on time. But all the while we want

to love each other endlessly—not only for
a hundred years, not only six feet up and down.
We want the suns and moons of silver
in ourselves, not only counted coins in a cup. The whole

idea of love was not to fall. And neither was
the whole idea of God. We put him well
above ourselves, because we meant,
in time, to measure up.

Things

Lisel Mueller

What happened is, we grew lonely
living among the things,
so we gave the clock a face,
the chair a back,
the table four stout legs
which will never suffer fatigue.

We fitted our shoes with tongues
as smooth as our own
and hung tongues inside bells
so we could listen
to their emotional language,

and because we loved graceful profiles
the pitcher received a lip,
the bottle a long, slender neck.

Even what was beyond us
was recast in our image;
we gave the country a heart,
the storm an eye,
the cave a mouth
so we could pass into safety.

Any prince to any princess

Adrian Henri

August is coming
and the goose, I'm afraid,
is getting fat.
There have been
no golden eggs for some months now.
Straw has fallen well below market price
despite my frantic spinning
and the sedge is,
as you rightly point out,
withered.

I can't imagine how the pea
got under your mattress. I apologize
humbly. The chambermaid has, of course,
been sacked. As has the frog footman.
I understand that, during my recent fact-finding tour of the
    Golden River,
despite your nightly unavailing efforts,
he remained obstinately
froggish.

I hope that the Three Wishes granted by the General
    Assembly
will go some way towards redressing
this unfortunate recent sequence of events.
The fall in output from the shoe-factory, for example:
no one could have foreseen the work-to-rule

by the National Union of Elves. Not to mention the fact
that the court has been fast asleep
for the last six and a half years.

The matter of the poisoned apple has been taken up
by the Board of Trade: I think I can assure you
the incident will not be
repeated.

I can quite understand, in the circumstances,
your reluctance to let down
your golden tresses. However
I feel I must point out
that the weather isn't getting any better
and I already have a nasty chill
from waiting at the base
of the White Tower. You must see the absurdity of the
        situation.
Some of the courtiers are beginning to talk,
not to mention the humble villagers.
It's been three weeks now, and not even
a word.

Princess,
a cold, black wind
howls through our empty palace.
Dead leaves litter the bedchamber;
the mirror on the wall hasn't said a thing
since you left. I can only ask,
bearing all this in mind,
that you think again,

let down your hair,

reconsider.

The courage that my mother had

Edna St. Vincent Millay

The courage that my mother had
Went with her, and is with her still:
Rock from New England quarried;
Now granite in a granite hill.

The golden brooch my mother wore
She left behind for me to wear;
I have no thing I treasure more:
Yet, it is something I could spare.

Oh, if instead she'd left to me
The thing she took into the grave!—
That courage like a rock, which she
Has no more need of, and I have.

Please Mrs Butler

Allan Ahlberg

Please Mrs Butler
This boy Derek Drew
Keeps copying my work, Miss.
What shall I do?

Go and sit in the hall, dear.
Go and sit in the sink.
Take your books on the roof, my lamb.
Do whatever you think.

Please Mrs Butler
This boy Derek Drew
Keeps taking my rubber, Miss.
What shall I do?

Keep it in your hand, dear.
Hide it up your vest.
Swallow it if you like, my love.
Do what you think best.

Please Mrs Butler
This boy Derek Drew
Keeps calling me rude names, Miss.
What shall I do?

Lock yourself in the cupboard, dear.
Run away to sea.
Do whatever you can, my flower.
But *don't ask me!*

To A Frustrated Poet

R. J. Ellmann

This is to say
I know
You wish you were in the woods,
Living the poet life,
Not here at a formica topped table
In a meeting about perceived inequalities in the benefits and
    allowances offered to employees of this college,
And I too wish you were in the woods,
Because it's no fun having a frustrated poet
In the Dept. of Human Resources, believe me.
In the poems of yours that I've read, you seem ever intelligent
    and decent and patient in a way
Not evident to us in this office,
And so, knowing how poets can make a feast out of trouble,
Raising flowers in a bed of drunkenness, divorce, despair,
I give you this check representing two weeks' wages
And ask you to clean out your desk today
And go home
And write a poem
With a real frog in it
And plums from the refrigerator,
So sweet and so cold.

the lesson of the moth

Don Marquis

i was talking to a moth
the other evening
he was trying to break into
an electric light bulb
and fry himself on the wires

why do you fellows
pull this stunt i asked him
because it is the conventional
thing for moths or why
if that had been an uncovered
candle instead of an electric
light bulb you would
now be a small unsightly cinder
have you no sense

plenty of it he answered
but at times we get tired
of using it
we get bored with the routine
and crave beauty
and excitement
fire is beautiful
and we know that if we get
too close it will kill us
but what does that matter

it is better to be happy
for a moment
and be burned up with beauty
than to live a long time
and be bored all the while
so we wad all our life up
into one little roll
and then we shoot the roll
that is what life is for
it is better to be a part of beauty
for one instant and then cease to
exist than to exist forever
and never be a part of beauty
our attitude toward life
is come easy go easy
we are like human beings
used to be before they became
too civilized to enjoy themselves

and before i could argue him
out of his philosophy
he went and immolated himself
on a patent cigar lighter
i do not agree with him
myself i would rather have
half the happiness and twice
the longevity

but at the same time i wish
there was something i wanted
as badly as he wanted to fry himself

Disappointment

Tony Hoagland

I was feeling pretty religious
standing on the bridge in my winter coat
looking down at the gray water:
the sharp little waves dusted with snow,
fish in their tin armor.

That's what I like about disappointment:
the way it slows you down,
when the querulous insistent chatter of desire
              goes dead calm

and the minor roadside flowers
pronounce their quiet colors,
and the red dirt of the hillside glows.

She played the flute, he played the fiddle
and the moon came up over the barn.
Then he didn't get the job,—
or her father died before she told him
              that one, most important thing—

and everything got still.

It was February or October
It was July
I remember it so clear
You don't have to pursue anything ever again
It's over
You're free
You're unemployed

You just have to stand there
looking out on the water
in your trench coat of solitude
with your scarf of resignation
                    lifting in the wind.

The Cure

Ginger Andrews

Lying around all day
with some strange new deep blue
weekend funk, I'm not really asleep
when my sister calls
to say she's just hung up
from talking with Aunt Bertha
who is 89 and ill but managing
to take care of Uncle Frank
who is completely bed ridden.
Aunt Bert says
it's snowing there in Arkansas,
on Catfish Lane, and she hasn't been
able to walk out to their mailbox.
She's been suffering
from a bad case of the mulleygrubs.
The cure for the mulleygrubs,
she tells my sister,
is to get up and bake a cake.
If that doesn't do it, put on a red dress.

Upon Hearing About the Suicide
of the Daughter of Friends

Jo McDougall

Something called to her that Sunday afternoon, perhaps,
that she could not name.
You and I cannot name it, drawn to each other
by this news.
The young cry when they feel it
breathing beside them.
We may know it sometimes through its disguises,
say the sound of a car at two a.m.
grinding to a stop in a gravel drive.

6

HERE IT COMES

the con job

Charles Bukowski

the ground war began today
at dawn
in a desert land
far from here.
the U.S. ground troops were
largely
made up of
Blacks, Mexicans and poor
whites
most of whom had joined
the military
because it was the only job
they could find.

the ground war began today
at dawn
in a desert land
far from here
and the Blacks, Mexicans
and poor whites
were sent there
to fight and win
as on tv
and on the radio
the fat white rich newscasters

first told us all about
it
and then the fat rich white
analysts
told us
why
again
and again
and again
on almost every
tv and radio station
almost every minute
day and night
because
the Blacks, Mexicans
and poor whites
were sent there
to fight and win
at dawn
in a desert land
far enough away from
here.

Fareweel to A' Our Scottish Fame

Robert Burns

Fareweel to a' our Scottish fame,
    Fareweel our ancient glory!
Fareweel even to the Scottish name,
    Sae fam'd in martial story!
Now Sark rins o'er Solway sands,
    And Tweed rins to the ocean,
To mark where England's province stands;
    Such a parcel of rogues in a nation!

What guile or force could not subdue,
    Through many warlike ages,
Is wrought now by a coward few,
    For hireling traitors' wages.
The English steel we could disdain,
    Secure in valour's station,
But English gold has been our bane;
    Such a parcel of rogues in a nation!

O would, ere I had seen the day
    That treason thus could sell us,
My auld grey head had lien in clay,
    Wi' Bruce and loyal Wallace!
But pith and power, till my last hour
    I'll mak this declaration,
We're bought and sold for English gold:
    Such a parcel of rogues in a nation!

Easter Morning

Jim Harrison

On Easter morning all over America
the peasants are frying potatoes in bacon grease.

We're not supposed to have "peasants"
but there are tens of millions of them
frying potatoes on Easter morning,
cheap and delicious with catsup.

If Jesus were here this morning he might
be eating fried potatoes with my friend
who has a '51 Dodge and a '72 Pontiac.

When his kids ask why they don't have
a new car he says, "these cars were new once
and now they are experienced."

He can fix anything and when rich folks
call to get a toilet repaired he pauses
extra hours so that they can further
learn what we're made of.

I told him that in Mexico the poor say
that when there's lightning the rich
think that God is taking their picture.
He laughed.

Like peasants everywhere in the history
of the world ours can't figure out why
they're getting poorer. Their sons join
the army to get work being shot at.

Your ideals are invisible clouds
so try not to suffocate the poor,
the peasants, with your sympathies.
They know that you're staring at them.

A Million Young Workmen, 1915

Carl Sandburg

A million young workmen straight and strong lay stiff on the
grass and roads,
And the million are now under soil and their rottening flesh will
in the years feed roots of blood-red roses.
Yes, this million of young workmen slaughtered one another and
never saw their red hands.
And oh, it would have been a great job of killing and a new and
beautiful thing under the sun if the million knew why they
hacked and tore each other to death.
The kings are grinning, the kaiser and the czar—they are alive
riding in leather-seated motor cars, and they have their
women and roses for ease, and they eat fresh poached eggs
for breakfast, new butter on toast, sitting in tall water-tight
houses reading the news of war.
I dreamed a million ghosts of the young workmen rose in their
shirts all soaked in crimson . . . and yelled:
God damn the grinning kings, God damn the kaiser and the czar.

The College Colonel.

Herman Melville

He rides at their head;
  A crutch by his saddle just slants in view,
One slung arm is in splints you see,
  Yet he guides his strong steed—how coldly too.

He brings his regiment home—
  Not as they filed two years before,
But a remnant half-tattered, and battered, and worn,
Like castaway sailors, who—stunned
    By the surf's loud roar,
  Their mates dragged back and seen no more—
Again and again breast the surge,
  And at last crawl, spent, to shore.

A still rigidity and pale—
  An Indian aloofness lones his brow;
He has lived a thousand years
Compressed in battle's pains and prayers,
  Marches and watches slow.

There are welcoming shouts, and flags;
  Old men off hat to the Boy,
Wreaths from gay balconies fall at his feet,
  But to *him*—there comes alloy.

It is not that a leg is lost,
　It is not that an arm is maimed,
It is not that the fever has racked—
　Self he has long disclaimed.

But all through the Seven Days' Fight,
　And deep in the Wilderness grim,
And in the field-hospital tent,
　And Petersburg crater, and dim
Lean brooding in Libby, there came—
　Ah heaven!—what *truth* to him.

Ordinary Life

Barbara Crooker

This was a day when nothing happened,
the children went off to school
without a murmur, remembering
their books, lunches, gloves.
All morning, the baby and I built block stacks
in the squares of light on the floor.
And lunch blended into naptime,
I cleaned out kitchen cupboards,
one of those jobs that never gets done,
then sat in a circle of sunlight
and drank ginger tea,
watched the birds at the feeder
jostle over lunch's little scraps.
A pheasant strutted from the hedgerow,
preened and flashed his jeweled head.
Now a chicken roasts in the pan,
and the children return,
the murmur of their stories dappling the air.
I peel carrots and potatoes without paring my thumb.
We listen together for your wheels on the drive.
Grace before bread.
And at the table, actual conversation,
no bickering or pokes.
And then, the drift into homework.
The baby goes to his cars, drives them
along the sofa's ridges and hills.

Leaning by the counter, we steal a long slow kiss,
tasting of coffee and cream.
The chicken's diminished to skin & skeleton,
the moon to a comma, a sliver of white,
but this has been a day of grace
in the dead of winter,
the hard cold knuckle of the year,
a day that unwrapped itself
like an unexpected gift,
and the stars turn on,
order themselves
into the winter night.

To fight aloud, is very brave

Emily Dickinson

To fight aloud, is very brave—
But *gallanter*, I know
Who charge within the bosom
The Cavalry of Woe—

Who win, and nations do not see—
Who fall—and none observe—
Whose dying eyes, no Country
Regards with patriot love—

We trust, in plumed procession
For such, the Angels go—
Rank after Rank, with even feet—
And Uniforms of Snow.

Analysis of Baseball

May Swenson

It's about
the ball,
the bat,
and the mitt.
Ball hits
bat, or it
hits mitt.
Bat doesn't
hit ball, bat
meets it.
Ball bounces
off bat, flies
air, or thuds
ground (dud)
or it
fits mitt.

Bat waits
for ball
to mate.
Ball hates
to take bat's
bait. Ball
flirts, bat's
late, don't
keep the date.

Ball goes in
(thwack) to mitt,
and goes out
(thwack) back
to mitt.

Ball fits
mitt, but
not all
the time.
Sometimes
ball gets hit
(pow) when bat
meets it,
and sails
to a place
where mitt
has to quit
in disgrace.
That's about
the bases
loaded,
about 40,000
fans exploded.

It's about
the ball,
the bat,
the mitt,
the bases
and the fans.

It's done
on a diamond,
and for fun.
It's about
home, and it's
about run.

Ode to American English

Barbara Hamby

I was missing English one day, American, really,
    with its pill-popping Hungarian goulash of everything
from Anglo-Saxon to Zulu, because British English
    is not the same, if the paperback dictionary
I bought at Brentano's on the Avenue de l'Opéra
    is any indication, too cultured by half. Oh, the English
know their dahlias, but what about doowop, donuts,
    Dick Tracy, Tricky Dick? With their elegant Oxfordian
accents, how could they understand my yearning for the hotrod,
    hotdog, hot flash vocabulary of the U. S. of A.,
the fragmented fandango of Dagwood's everyday flattening
    of Mr. Beasley on the sidewalk, fetuses floating
on billboards, drive-by monster hip-hop stereos shaking
    the windows of my dining room like a 7.5 earthquake,
Ebonics, Spanglish, "you know" used as comma and period,
    the inability of 90% of the population to get the present perfect:
I have went, I have saw, I have tooken Jesus into my heart,
    the battle cry of the Bible Belt, but no one uses
the King James anymore, only plain-speak versions,
    in which Jesus, raising Lazarus from the dead, says,
"Dude, wake up," and the L-man bolts up like a B-movie
    mummy. "Whoa, I was toasted." Yes, ma'am,
I miss the mongrel plentitude of American English, its fall-guy,
    rat-terrier, dog-pound neologisms, the bomb of it all,
the rushing River Jordan backwoods mutability of it, the low-rider,
    boom-box cruise of it, from New Joisey to Ha-wah-ya

with its sly dog, malasada-scarfing beach blanket lingo
　　　to the ubiquitous Valley Girl's *like-like* stuttering,
shopaholic rant. I miss its quotidian beauty, its querulous
　　　back-biting righteous indignation, its preening rotgut
flag-waving cowardice. *Suffering Succotash*, sputters
　　　Sylvester the Cat; *sine die*, say the pork-bellied legislators
of the swamps and plains. I miss all those guys, their Tweety-bird
　　　resilience, their Doris Day optimism, the candid unguent
of utter unhappiness on every channel, the midnight televangelist
　　　euphoric stew, the junk mail, voice mail vernacular.
On every *boulevard* and *rue* I miss the Tarzan cry of Johnny
　　　Weismueller, Johnny Cash, Johnny B. Goode,
and all the smart-talking, gum-snapping hard-girl dialogue,
　　　finger-popping x-rated street talk, sports babble,
Cheetoes, Cheerios, chili dog diatribes. Yeah, I miss them all,
　　　sitting here on my sidewalk throne sipping champagne
verses lined up like hearses, metaphors juking, nouns zipping
　　　in my head like Corvettes on Dexedrine, French verbs
slitting my throat, yearning for James Dean to jump my curb.

High Water Mark

David Shumate

It's hard to believe, but at one point the water rose to this
level. No one had seen anything like it. People on rooftops.
Cows and coffins floating through the streets. Prisoners
carrying invalids from their rooms. The barkeeper consoling
the preacher. A coon hound who showed up a month later
forty miles downstream. And all that mud it left behind. You
never forget times like those. They become part of who you
are. You describe them to your grandchildren. But they think
it's just another tale in which animals talk and people live
forever. I know it's not the kind of thing you ought to say . . .
But I wouldn't mind seeing another good flood before I die.
It's been dry for decades. Next time I think I'll just let go and
drift downstream and see where I end up.

After School on Ordinary Days

Maria Mazziotti Gillan

After school on ordinary days we listened
to *The Shadow* and *The Lone Ranger*
as we gathered around the tabletop radio
that was always kept on the china cabinet
built into the wall in that tenement kitchen,
a china cabinet that held no china, except
thick and white and utilitarian,
cups and saucers, poor people's cups
from the 5 & 10 cent store.
My mother was always home
from Ferraro's Coat factory
by the time we walked in the door
after school on ordinary days,
and she'd give us milk with Bosco in it
and cookies she'd made that weekend.
The three of us would crowd around the radio,
listening to the voices that brought a wider world
into our Paterson apartment. Later

we'd have supper at the kitchen table,
the house loud with our arguments
and laughter. After supper on ordinary
days, our homework finished, we'd play
monopoly or gin rummy, the kitchen
warmed by the huge coal stove, the wind
outside rattling the loose old windows,
we inside, tucked in, warm and together,
on ordinary days that we didn't know
until we looked back across a distance
of forty years would glow and shimmer
in memory's flickering light.

Snow in the Suburbs

Thomas Hardy

Every branch big with it,
  Bent every twig with it;
Every fork like a white web-foot;
Every street and pavement mute:
Some flakes have lost their way, and grope back upward,
                              when
Meeting those meandering down they turn and descend
                              again.
  The palings are glued together like a wall,
  And there is no waft of wind with the fleecy fall.

  A sparrow enters the tree,
  Whereon immediately
A snow-lump thrice his own slight size
Descends on him and showers his head and eyes,
    And overturns him,
    And near inurns him,
  And lights on a nether twig, when its brush
Starts off a volley of other lodging lumps with a rush.

  The steps are a blanched slope,
  Up which, with feeble hope,
  A black cat comes, wide-eyed and thin;
    And we take him in.

Now Winter Nights Enlarge

Thomas Campion

Now winter nights enlarge
   The number of their houres,
And clouds their stormes discharge
   Upon the ayrie towres:
Let now the chimneys blaze,
   And cups o'erflow with wine:
Let well-tun'd words amaze
   With harmonie divine.
Now yellow waxen lights
   Shall waite on hunny Love,
While youthfull Revels, Masks, and Courtly sights,
   Sleepes leaden spels remove.

This time doth well dispence
   With lovers long discourse;
Much speech hath some defence,
   Though beauty no remorse.
All doe not all things well;
   Some measures comely tread,
Some knotted Ridles tell,
   Some Poems smoothly read.
The Summer hath his joyes,
   And Winter his delights;
Though Love and all his pleasures are but toyes,
   They shorten tedious nights.

Happiness

Michael Van Walleghen

"Weep for what little things could make them glad."
—"DIRECTIVE," ROBERT FROST

Melvin,
    the large collie
who lives in the red house
at the end of my daily run
is happy,
    happy to see me
even now,
    in February—
a month of low skies
and slowly melting snow.

His yard
    has turned almost
entirely to mud—
        but so what?

Today,
    as if to please me,
he has torn apart
        and scattered
everywhere
        a yellow plastic bucket
the color of forsythia
or daffodils . . .

And now,
in a transport
    of cross-eyed
muddy ecstasy,
    he has placed
his filthy two front paws
together
    on the top pipe
of his sagging cyclone fence—

drooling a little,
    his tail
wagging furiously,
    until finally,
as if I were God's angel himself—

fulgent,
    blinding,
        aflame
with news of the Resurrection,
I give him a biscuit
    instead.

Which is fine with Melvin—
who is wise,
    by whole epochs
of evolution,
    beyond his years.

Take
    what you can get,
that's his motto . . .

                    And really,
            apropos of bliss,
                    happiness
            and the true rapture,
                    what saint
            could tell us half as much?

            Even as he drops
                    back down
            into the cold
                    dog-shit muck
            he'll have to live in
                    every day
            for weeks on end perhaps
            unless it freezes . . .

            whining now,
                dancing
            nervously
                as I turn away
            again,
                to leave him there

            the same today
                    as yesterday—

            one of the truly wretched
            of this earth
                whose happiness
            is almost more
                    than I can bear.

from Tender Buttons

Gertrude Stein

A light in the moon the only light is on Sunday. What was the sensible decision. The sensible decision was that notwithstanding many declarations and more music, not even notwithstanding the choice and a torch and a collection, notwithstanding the celebrating hat and a vacation and even more noise than cutting, notwithstanding Europe and Asia and being overbearing, not even notwithstanding an elephant and a strict occasion, not even withstanding more cultivation and some seasoning, not even with drowning and with the ocean being encircling, not even with more likeness and any cloud, not even with terrific sacrifice of pedestrianism and a special resolution, not even more likely to be pleasing. The care with which the rain is wrong and the green is wrong and the white is wrong, the care with which there is a chair and plenty of breathing. The care with which there is incredible justice and likeness, all this makes a magnificent asparagus, and also a fountain.

Classic Ballroom Dances

Charles Simic

Grandmothers who wring the necks
Of chickens; old nuns
With names like Theresa, Marianne,
Who pull schoolboys by the ear;

The intricate steps of pickpockets
Working the crowd of the curious
At the scene of an accident; the slow shuffle
Of the evangelist with a sandwich-board;

The hesitation of the early morning customer
Peeking through the window-grille
Of a pawnshop; the weave of a little kid
Who is walking to school with eyes closed;

And the ancient lovers, cheek to cheek,
On the dancefloor of the Union Hall,
Where they also hold charity raffles
On rainy Monday nights of an eternal November.

Theater

William Greenway

Like the neighborhood kind
you went to as a kid, full
of yellow light and red
velvet curtains and everybody
there, friends, bullies throwing
popcorn, somebody with red hair.
The roof is leak-stained like the bloody
footprints of the beast from 20,000 fathoms,
there's a yo-yo demonstration by
a greasy man in a sequined suit,
the girl you love is there somewhere
but you can't find her, or if you do
she's with some jerk with muscles.
And the show won't start. There's whistling
and stomping, paper airplanes and 3-D
glasses until you don't even care
anymore because your head is tired,
a stone atop a tendril, and you just
want to sleep, when, sure enough,
the curtain finally rises,
darkness falls,
and here it comes.

Ode on the Whole Duty Of Parents

Frances Cornford

The spirits of children are remote and wise,
They must go free
Like fishes in the sea
Or starlings in the skies,
Whilst you remain
The shore where casually they come again.
But when there falls the stalking shade of fear,
You must be suddenly near,
You, the unstable, must become a tree
In whose unending heights of flowering green
Hangs every fruit that grows, with silver bells;
Where heart-distracting magic birds are seen
And all the things a fairy-story tells;
Though still you should possess
Roots that go deep in ordinary earth,
And strong consoling bark
To love and to caress.

Last, when at dark
Safe on the pillow lies an up-gazing head
And drinking holy eyes
Are fixed on you,
When, from behind them, questions come to birth
Insistently,
On all the things that you have ever said
Of suns and snakes and parallelograms and flies,
And whether these are true,
Then for a while you'll need to be no more
That sheltering shore
Or legendary tree in safety spread,
No, then you must put on
The robes of Solomon,
Or simply be
Sir Isaac Newton sitting on the bed.

7

WHATEVER HAPPENS

The Benefits of Ignorance

Hal Sirowitz

If ignorance is bliss, Father said,
shouldn't you be looking blissful?
You should check to see if you have
the right kind of ignorance. If you're
not getting the benefits that most people
get from acting stupid, then you should
go back to what you always were—
being too smart for your own good.

Bunthorne's Song

(from *Patience*)

W. S. Gilbert

If you're anxious for to shine
in the high aesthetic line
as a man of culture rare,
You must get up all the germs
of the transcendental terms,
and plant them everywhere.
You must lie upon the daisies
and discourse in novel phrases
of your complicated state of mind.
The meaning doesn't matter if it's only idle chatter
of a transcendental kind.
And every one will say,
As you walk your mystic way,
'If this young man expresses himself
in terms too deep for *me*,
Why, what a very singularly deep young man
this deep young man must be!'

Be eloquent in praise of the very dull old days
which have long since passed away,
And convince 'em, if you can, that the reign
of good Queen Anne was Culture's palmiest day.
Of course you will pooh-pooh whatever's fresh and new,
and declare it's crude and mean,

For Art stopped short in the cultivated court
of the Empress Josephine.
And every one will say,
As you walk your mystic way,
'If that's not good enough for him
which is good enough for *me*,
Why, what a very cultivated kind
of youth this kind of youth must be!'

Then a sentimental passion of a vegetable fashion
must excite your languid spleen,
An attachment *à la Plato* for a bashful young potato,
or a not-too-French French bean!
Though the Philistines may jostle, you will rank
as an apostle in the high aesthetic band,
If you walk down Piccadilly with a poppy
or a lily in your medieval hand.
And every one will say
As you walk your flowery way,
'If he's content with a vegetable love
which would certainly not suit *me*,
Why, what a most particularly pure young man
this pure young man must be!'

The Rules of Evidence

Lee Robinson

What you want to say most
is inadmissible.
Say it anyway.
Say it again.
What they tell you is irrelevant
can't be denied and will
eventually be heard.
Every question
is a leading question.
Ask it anyway, then expect
what you won't get.
There is no such thing
as the original
so you'll have to make do
with a reasonable facsimile.
The history of the world
is hearsay. Hear it.
The whole truth
is unspeakable
and nothing but the truth
is a lie.
I swear this.
My oath is a kiss.
I swear
by everything
incredible.

Courtesy

Hilaire Belloc

Of Courtesy, it is much less
Than Courage of Heart or Holiness,
Yet in my Walks it seems to me
That the Grace of God is in Courtesy.

On Monks I did in Storrington fall,
They took me straight into their Hall;
I saw Three Pictures on a wall,
And Courtesy was in them all.

The first the Annunciation;
The second the Visitation;
The third the Consolation,
Of God that was Our Lady's Son.

The first was of Saint Gabriel;
On Wings a-flame from Heaven he fell;
And as he went upon one knee
He shone with Heavenly Courtesy.

Our Lady out of Nazareth rode—
It was Her month of heavy load;
Yet was Her face both great and kind,
For Courtesy was in Her Mind.

The third it was our Little Lord,
Whom all the Kings in arms adored;
He was so small you could not see
His large intent of Courtesy.

Our Lord, that was Our Lady's Son,
Go bless you, People, one by one;
My Rhyme is written, my work is done.

What the Uneducated Old Woman Told Me

Christopher Reid

That she was glad to sit down.

That her legs hurt in spite of the medicine.

That times were bad.

That her husband had died nearly thirty years before.

That the war had changed things.

That the new priest looked like a schoolboy and you could
barely hear him in church.

That pigs were better company, generally speaking, than goats.

That no one could fool her.

That both her sons had married stupid women.

That her son-in-law drove a truck.

That he had once delivered something to the President's palace.

That his flat was on the seventh floor and that it made her dizzy
to think of it.

That he brought her presents from the black market.

That an alarm clock was of no use to her.

That she could no longer walk to town and back.

That all her friends were dead.

That I should be careful about mushrooms.

That ghosts never came to a house where a sprig of rosemary had
been hung.

That the cinema was a ridiculous invention.

That the modern dances were no good.

That her husband had had a beautiful singing voice, until drink
ruined it.

That the war had changed things.

That she had seen on a map where the war had been fought.
That Hitler was definitely in Hell right now.
That children were cheekier than ever.
That it was going to be a cold winter, you could tell from the
    height of the birds' nests.
That even salt was expensive these days.
That she had had a long life and was not afraid of dying.
That times were very bad.

Proverbs of Hell

William Blake

In seed time learn, in harvest teach, in winter enjoy.
Drive your cart and your plough over the bones of the dead.
The road of excess leads to the palace of wisdom.
A fool sees not the same tree that a wise man sees.
He whose face gives no light shall never become a star.
Eternity is in love with the productions of time.
The busy bee has no time for sorrow.
The hours of folly are measured by the clock,
  but of wisdom no clock can measure.
All wholesome food is caught without a net or a trap.
The fox condemns the trap, not himself.
Joys impregnate. Sorrows bring forth.
What is now proved was once only imagined.
The rat, the mouse, the fox, the rabbit, watch the roots. The lion,
  the tiger, the horse, the elephant, watch the fruits.
The cistern contains; the fountain overflows.
One thought fills immensity.
Think in the morning; act in the noon; eat in the evening;
  sleep in the night.
You never know what is enough unless you know
  what is more than enough.
Listen to the fool's reproach! It is a kingly title!
The eyes of fire, the nostrils of air, the mouth of water,
  the beard of earth.
The thankful receiver bears a plentiful harvest.
If others had not been foolish, we should be so.

The soul of sweet delight can never be defiled.
When thou seest an eagle, thou seest a portion of genius;
   lift up thy head!
Exuberance is beauty.
If the lion was advised by the fox, he would be cunning.
Improvement makes straight roads, but the crooked roads
   without improvement are roads of genius.
      Enough! Or too much!
The ancient poets animated all sensible objects with gods or
   geniuses, calling them by the names, and adorning them with
   the properties of woods, rivers, mountains, lakes, cities, nations,
   and whatever their enlarged and numerous senses could per-
   ceive.
And particularly they studied the genius of each city and country,
   placing it under its mental deity.
Till a system was formed, which some took advantage of and
   enslaved the vulgar by attempting to realise or abstract the
   mental deities from their objects. Thus began priesthood:
   choosing forms of worship from poetic tales.
And at length they pronounced that the gods had ordered such
   things.
Thus men forgot that all deities reside in the human breast.

To a Daughter Leaving Home

Linda Pastan

When I taught you
at eight to ride
a bicycle, loping along
beside you
as you wobbled away
on two round wheels,
my own mouth rounding
in surprise when you pulled
ahead down the curved
path of the park,
I kept waiting
for the thud
of your crash as I
sprinted to catch up,
while you grew
smaller, more breakable
with distance,
pumping, pumping
for your life, screaming
with laughter,
the hair flapping
behind you like a
handkerchief waving
goodbye.

No Longer A Teenager

Gerald Locklin

my daughter, who turns twenty tomorrow,
has become truly independent.
she doesn't need her father to help her
deal with the bureaucracies of schools,
hmo's, insurance, the dmv.
she is quite capable of handling
landlords, bosses, and auto repair shops.
also boyfriends and roommates.
and her mother.

frankly it's been a big relief.
the teenage years were often stressful.
sometimes, though, i feel a little useless.

but when she drove down from northern California
to visit us for a couple of days,
she came through the door with the
biggest, warmest hug in the world for me.
and when we all went out for lunch,
she said, affecting a little girl's voice,
"i'm going to sit next to my daddy,"
and she did, and slid over close to me
so i could put my arm around her shoulder
until the food arrived.

i've been keeping busy since she's been gone,
mainly with my teaching and writing,
a little travel connected with both,
but i realized now how long it had been
since i had felt deep emotion.

when she left i said, simply,
"i love you,"
and she replied, quietly,
"i love you too."
you know it isn't always easy for
a twenty-year-old to say that;
it isn't always easy for a father.

literature and opera are full of
characters who die for love:
i stay alive for her.

Prayer

Galway Kinnell

Whatever happens. Whatever
what is is is what
I want. Only that. But that.

Minnesota Thanksgiving

John Berryman

For that free Grace bringing us past great risks
& thro' great griefs surviving to this feast
sober & still, with the children unborn and born,
among brave friends, Lord, we stand again in debt
and find ourselves in the glad position: Gratitude.

We praise our ancestors who delivered us here
within warm walls all safe, aware of music,
likely toward ample & attractive meat
with whatever accompaniment
Kate in her kind ingenuity has seen fit to devise,

and we hope—across the most strange year to come—
continually to do them and You not sufficient honour
but such as we become able to devise
out of decent or joyful *conscience* & thanksgiving.
Yippee!
          Bless then, as Thou wilt, this wilderness board.

Berryman

W. S. Merwin

I will tell you what he told me
in the years just after the war
as we then called
the second world war

don't lose your arrogance yet he said
you can do that when you're older
lose it too soon and you may
merely replace it with vanity

just one time he suggested
changing the usual order
of the same words in a line of verse
why point out a thing twice

he suggested I pray to the Muse
get down on my knees and pray
right there in the corner and he
said he meant it literally

it was in the days before the beard
and the drink but he was deep
in tides of his own through which he sailed
chin sideways and head tilted like a tacking sloop

he was far older than the dates allowed for
much older than I was he was in his thirties
he snapped down his nose with an accent
I think he had affected in England

as for publishing he advised me
to paper my wall with rejection slips
his lips and the bones of his long fingers trembled
with the vehemence of his views about poetry

he said the great presence
that permitted everything and transmuted it
in poetry was passion
passion was genius and he praised movement and invention

I had hardly begun to read
I asked how can you ever be sure
that what you write is really
any good at all and he said you can't

you can't you can never be sure
you die without knowing
whether anything you wrote was any good
if you have to be sure don't write

Mother, in Love at Sixty

Susanna Styve

Reason number one it can't work: his name is Bill. For god's
sake, he hunts. He has no pets, other than two doting
daughters, and his ex-wife is still alive. He's simply not my
type. Who wants to get married again, anyway? I'm too old.
I go South at the first frost. Plus, he's messy. Men are messy.
He could die. Then where would I be?

My Agent Says

R. S. Gwynn

My agent says Los Angeles will call.
My broker says to sell without delay.
My doctor says the spot is very small.
My lover says get tested right away.

My congressman says yes, he truly cares.
My bottle says he'll see me after five.
My mirror says to pluck a few stray hairs.
My mother says that she is still alive.

My leader says we may have seen the worst.
My mistress says her eyes are like the sun.
My bride says that it's true I'm not the first.
My landlord says he'd think about a gun.

My boss says that I'd better take a chair.
My enemy says turn the other cheek.
My rival says that all in love is fair.
My brother says he's coming for a week.

My teacher says my work is very neat.
My ex-wife says I haven't heard the last.
My usher says the big guy's in my seat.
My captain says to bind him to the mast.

My master says I must be taught my place.
My conscience says my schemes will never fly.
My father says he doesn't like my face.
My lawyer says I shouldn't testify.

My buddy says this time I've got it bad.
My first love says she can't recall my name.
My baby says my singing makes her sad.
My dog says that she loves me all the same.

My pastor says to walk the narrow path.
My coach says someone else will get the ball.
My God says I shall bend beneath His wrath.
My agent says Los Angeles may call.

Afraid So

Jeanne Marie Beaumont

Is it starting to rain?
Did the check bounce?
Are we out of coffee?
Is this going to hurt?
Could you lose your job?
Did the glass break?
Was the baggage misrouted?
Will this go on my record?
Are you missing much money?
Was anyone injured?
Is the traffic heavy?
Do I have to remove my clothes?
Will it leave a scar?
Must you go?
Will this be in the papers?
Is my time up already?
Are we seeing the understudy?
Will it affect my eyesight?
Did all the books burn?
Are you still smoking?
Is the bone broken?
Will I have to put him to sleep?
Was the car totaled?
Am I responsible for these charges?
Are you contagious?
Will we have to wait long?

Is the runway icy?
Was the gun loaded?
Could this cause side effects?
Do you know who betrayed you?
Is the wound infected?
Are we lost?
Will it get any worse?

The Yak

Hilaire Belloc

As a friend to the children
      commend me the Yak.
   You will find it exactly the thing:
It will carry and fetch,
      you can ride on its back,
Or lead it about
      with a string.
The Tartar who dwells on the plains of Thibet
   (A desolate region of snow)
Has for centuries made it a nursery pet,
   And surely the Tartar should know!
Then tell your papa where the Yak can be got
   And if he is awfully rich
He will buy you the creature—
      or else
        he will *not*.
(I cannot be positive which.)

High Plains Farming

William Notter

There's never enough of the right kind of rain,
and always too much of what we get.
We've got no need for casinos—
keeping the farm is enough to gamble on.
If the seed doesn't blow out of the ground in December,
the wheat gets laid down flat in the fields by hail
come summer. Spring blizzards get the calves,
and one year my corn was nothing
but rows of stalks from softball-size hail
a month before harvest. That storm ruined my shingles
and beat the siding right off the neighbors' house.

A little hail and wind can't run me off, though,
and I'll keep dropping the well until the aquifer
dries up like they've said it would for years.
We may not know what it's going to leave us with,
but we can see our weather coming.
When those fronts blow across the fields,
trailing dust and rain, we've got time
to get the cars in the shed, and ourselves
into the basement if the clouds are green.

Next morning I go out to see where the dice fell.
Everything's glazed and bright with the dust knocked off
and the sun barely up. The gravel on the roads
is clean-washed pink, and water still hangs
on the fence wires and the pasture grass.
Sometimes I need to call the county
about a washed-out road, or the insurance man
about a field stripped clean. When I'm lucky
I can shut the irrigation pumps down
for a day or two and give the well a rest.

I like to drive right into it sometimes
when a storm comes up, lightning arcing
all directions over the hills, and the slate-blue
edge of the front clean as a section line.
There's an instant in that border
where it's not quite clear but not the storm
when everything seems to stop, like my wheels
have left the road. The light turns spooky, dust
just hangs, the grass glows like it's ready
to spark and catch on fire. Then the motor strains,
fat raindrops whack the tin and glass
like the racket from a flock of blackbirds,
hundreds of them scattering off a stubblefield.

The Fish

Elizabeth Bishop

I caught a tremendous fish
and held him beside the boat
half out of water, with my hook
fast in a corner of his mouth.
He didn't fight.
He hadn't fought at all.
He hung a grunting weight,
battered and venerable
and homely. Here and there
his brown skin hung like strips
like ancient wallpaper,
and its pattern of darker brown
was like wallpaper:
shapes like full-blown roses
stained and lost through age.
He was speckled with barnacles,
fine rosettes of lime,
and infested
with tiny white sea-lice,
and underneath two or three
rags of green weed hung down.
While his gills were breathing in
the terrible oxygen
—the frightening gills,
fresh and crisp with blood,
that can cut so badly—

I thought of the coarse white flesh
packed in like feathers,
the big bones and the little bones,
the dramatic reds and blacks
of his shiny entrails,
and the pink swim-bladder
like a big peony.
I looked into his eyes
which were far larger than mine
but shallower, and yellowed,
the irises backed and packed
with tarnished tinfoil
seen through the lenses
of old scratched isinglass.
They shifted a little, but not
to return my stare.
—It was more like the tipping
of an object toward the light.
I admired his sullen face,
the mechanism of his jaw,
and then I saw
that from his lower lip
—if you could call it a lip—
grim, wet, and weaponlike,
hung five old pieces of fish-line,
or four and a wire leader
with the swivel still attached,
with all their five big hooks
grown firmly in his mouth.
A green line, frayed at the end
where he broke it, two heavier lines,
and a fine black thread
still crimped from the strain and snap
when it broke and he got away.

Like medals with their ribbons
frayed and wavering,
a five-haired beard of wisdom
trailing from his aching jaw.
I stared and stared
and victory filled up
the little rented boat,
from the pool of bilge
where oil had spread a rainbow
around the rusted engine
to the bailer rusted orange,
the sun-cracked thwarts,
the oarlocks on their strings,
the gunnels—until everything
was rainbow, rainbow, rainbow!
And I let the fish go.

The Future

Wesley McNair

On the afternoon talk shows of America
the guests have suffered life's sorrows
long enough. All they require now
is the opportunity for closure,
to put the whole thing behind them
and get on with their lives. That their lives,
in fact, are getting on with them even
as they announce their requirement
is written on the faces of the younger ones
wrinkling their brows, and the skin
of their elders collecting just under their
set chins. It's not easy to escape the past,
but who wouldn't want to live in a future
where the worst has already happened
and Americans can finally relax after daring
to demand a different way? For the rest of us,
the future, barring variations, turns out
to be not so different from the present
where we have always lived—the same
struggle of wishes and losses, and hope,
that old lieutenant, picking us up
every so often to dust us off and adjust
our helmets. Adjustment, for that matter,
may be the one lesson hope has to give,
serving us best when we begin to find
what we didn't know we wanted in what

the future brings. Nobody would have asked
for the ice storm that takes down trees
and knocks the power out, leaving nothing
but two buckets of snow melting
on the wood stove and candlelight so weak,
the old man sitting at the kitchen table
can hardly see to play cards. Yet how else
but by the old woman's laughter
when he mistakes a jack for a queen
would he look at her face in the half-light as if
for the first time while the kitchen around them
and the very cards he holds in his hands
disappear? In the deep moment of his looking
and her looking back, there is no future,
only right now, all, anyway, each one of us
has ever had, and all the two of them,
sitting together in the dark among the cracked
notes of the snow thawing beside them
on the stove, right now will ever need.

Riveted

Robyn Sarah

It is possible that things will not get better
than they are now, or have been known to be.
It is possible that we are past the middle now.
It is possible that we have crossed the great water
without knowing it, and stand now on the other side.
Yes: I think that we have crossed it. Now
we are being given tickets, and they are not
tickets to the show we had been thinking of,
but to a different show, clearly inferior.

Check again: it is our own name on the envelope.
The tickets are to that other show.

It is possible that we will walk out of the darkened hall
without waiting for the last act: people do.
Some people do. But it is probable
that we will stay seated in our narrow seats
all through the tedious dénouement
to the unsurprising end—riveted, as it were;
spellbound by our own imperfect lives
because they are lives,
and because they are ours.

All That Time

May Swenson

I saw two trees embracing.
One leaned on the other
as if to throw her down.
But she was the upright one.
Since their twin youth, maybe she
had been pulling him toward her
all that time,

and finally almost uprooted him.
He was the thin, dry, insecure one,
the most wind-warped, you could see.
And where their tops tangled
it looked like he was crying
on her shoulder.
On the other hand, maybe he

had been trying to weaken her,
break her, or at least
make her bend
over backwards for him
just a little bit.
And all that time
she was standing up to him

the best she could.
She was the most stubborn,
the straightest one, that's a fact.
But he had been willing
to change himself—
even if it was for the worse—
all that time.

At the top they looked like one
tree, where they were embracing.
It was plain they'd be
always together.

Too late now to part.
When the wind blew, you could hear
them rubbing on each other.

My Husband Discovers Poetry

Diane Lockward

Because my husband would not read my poems,
I wrote one about how I did not love him.
In lines of strict iambic pentameter,
I detailed his coldness, his lack of humor.
It felt good to do this.

Stanza by stanza, I grew bolder and bolder.
Towards the end, struck by inspiration,
I wrote about my old boyfriend,
a boy I had not loved enough to marry
but who could make me laugh and laugh.
I wrote about a night years after we parted
when my husband's coldness drove me from the house
and back to my old boyfriend.
I even included the name of a seedy motel
well-known for hosting quickies.
I have a talent for verisimilitude.

In sensuous images, I described
how my boyfriend and I stripped off our clothes,
got into bed, and kissed and kissed,
then spent half the night telling jokes,
many of them about my husband.
I left the ending deliberately ambiguous,
then hid the poem away
in an old trunk in the basement.

You know how this story ends,
how my husband one day loses something,
goes into the basement,
and rummages through the old trunk,
how he uncovers the hidden poem
and sits down to read it.

But do you hear the strange sounds
that floated up the stairs that day,
the sounds of an animal, its paw caught
in one of those traps with teeth of steel?
Do you see the wounded creature
at the bottom of the stairs,
his shoulders hunched over and shaking,
fist in his mouth and choking back sobs?
It was my husband paying tribute to my art.

The Poet's Occasional Alternative

Grace Paley

I was going to write a poem
I made a pie instead   it took
about the same amount of time
of course the pie was a final
draft   a poem would have had some
distance to go   days and weeks and
much crumpled paper

the pie already had a talking
tumbling audience among small
trucks and a fire engine on
the kitchen floor

everybody will like this pie
it will have apples and cranberries
dried apricots in it   many friends
will say   why in the world did you
make only one

this does not happen with poems

because of unreportable
sadnesses I decided to
settle this morning for a re-
sponsive eatership   I do not
want to wait a week   a year   a
generation for the right
consumer to come along

The Unsaid

Stephen Dunn

One night they both needed different things
of a similar kind; she, solace; he, to be consoled.
So after a wine-deepened dinner
when they arrived at their house separately
in the same car, each already had been failing
the other with what seemed
an unbearable delay of what felt due.
What solace meant to her was being understood
so well you'd give it to her before she asked.
To him, consolation was a network
of agreements: say what you will
as long as you acknowledge what I mean.
In the bedroom they undressed and dressed
and got into bed. The silence was what fills
a tunnel after a locomotive passes through.
Days later the one most needy finally spoke.
"What's on TV tonight?" he said this time,
and she answered, and they were okay again.
Each, forever, would remember the failure
to give solace, the failure to be consoled.
And many, many future nights
would find them turning to their respective sides
of the bed, terribly awake and twisting up
the covers, or, just as likely, moving closer
and sleeping forgetfully the night long.

Snapshot of a Lump

Kelli Russell Agodon

I imagine Nice and topless beaches,
women smoking and reading novels in the sun.
I pretend I am comfortable undressing
in front of men who go home to their wives,
in front of women who have seen
    twenty pairs of breasts today,
in front of silent ghosts who walked
    through these same doors before me,
who hoped doctors would find it soon enough,
    that surgery, pills and chemo could save them.

Today, they target my lump
with a small round sticker, a metal capsule
embedded beneath clear plastic.
I am asked to wash off my deodorant,
wrap a lead apron around my waist,
pose for the nurse, for the white walls—
one arm resting on the mammogram machine,
that "come hither" look in my eyes.
This is my first time being photographed topless.
I tell the nurse, *Will I be the centerfold*
or just another playmate?

My breast is pressed flat—a torpedo,
a pyramid, a triangle, a rocket on this altar;
this can't be good for anyone.
Finally, the nurse, winded
from fumbling, smiles,
says, "Don't breathe or move."
A flash and my breast is free,
but only for a moment.

In the waiting room, I sit between magazines,
an article on Venice,
health charts, people in white.
I pretend I am comfortable watching
other women escorted off to a side room,
where results are given with condolences.

I imagine leaving here
        with negative results and returned lives.
I imagine future trips to France,
        to novels I will write and days spent
beneath a blue and white sun umbrella,
waves washing against the shore like promises.

Hymn to God, my God, in my Sickness

John Donne

Since I am coming to that holy room,
    Where, with thy choir of saints for evermore,
I shall be made thy music; as I come
    I tune the instrument here at the door,
    And what I must do then, think here before.

Whilst my physicians by their love are grown
    Cosmographers, and I their map, who lie
Flat on this bed, that by them may be shown
    That this is my south-west discovery
    Per fretum febris, by these straits to die,

I joy, that in these straits, I see my west;
    For, though their currents yield return to none,
What shall my west hurt me? As west and east
    In all flat maps (and I am one) are one,
    So death doth touch the resurrection.

Is the Pacific Sea my home? Or are
    The eastern riches? Is Jerusalem?
Anyan, and Magellan, and Gibraltar,
    All straits, and none but straits, are ways to them,
    Whether where Japhet dwelt, or Cham, or Shem.

We think that Paradise and Calvary,
    Christ's Cross and Adam's tree, stood in one place;
Look Lord, and find both Adams met in me;
    As the first Adam's sweat surrounds my face,
May the last Adam's blood my soul embrace.

So, in his purple wrapped receive me Lord,
    By these his thorns give me his other crown;
And as to others' souls I preached thy word,
    Be this my text, my sermon to mine own,
    Therefore that he may raise the Lord throws down.

Last Days

Donald Hall

"It was reasonable
to expect." So he wrote. The next day,
    in a consultation room,
Jane's hematologist Letha Mills sat down,
    stiff, her assistant
standing with her back to the door.
    "I have terrible news,"
Letha told them. "The leukemia is back.
    There's nothing to do."
The four of them wept. He asked how long,
    why did it happen now?
Jane asked only: "Can I die at home?"

    Home that afternoon,
they threw her medicines into the trash.
    Jane vomited. He wailed
while she remained dry-eyed—silent,
    trying to let go. At night
he picked up the telephone to make
    calls that brought
a child or a friend into the horror.
    The next morning,
they worked choosing among her poems
    for *Otherwise*, picked
hymns for her funeral, and supplied each

other words as they wrote
and revised her obituary. The day after,
    with more work to do
on her book, he saw how weak she felt,
    and said maybe not now; maybe
later. Jane shook her head: "Now," she said.
    "We have to finish it now."
Later, as she slid exhausted into sleep,
    she said, "Wasn't that fun?
To work together? Wasn't that fun?"

    He asked her, "What clothes
should we dress you in, when we bury you?"
    "I hadn't thought," she said.
"I wondered about the white salwar
    kameez," he said—
her favorite Indian silk they bought
    in Pondicherry a year
and a half before, which she wore for best
    or prettiest afterward.
She smiled. "Yes. Excellent," she said.
    He didn't tell her
that a year earlier, dreaming awake,
    he had seen her
in the coffin in her white salwar kameez.

    Still, he couldn't stop
planning. That night he broke out with,
    "When Gus dies I'll
have him cremated and scatter his ashes
    on your grave!" She laughed
and her big eyes quickened and she nodded:

"It will be good
for the daffodils." She lay pallid back
        on the flowered pillow:
"Perkins, how do you *think* of these things?"

        They talked about their
adventures—driving through England
        when they first married,
and excursions to China and India.
        Also they remembered
ordinary days—pond summers, working
        on poems together,
walking the dog, reading Chekhov
        aloud. When he praised
thousands of afternoon assignations
        that carried them into
bliss and repose on this painted bed,
        Jane burst into tears
and cried, "No more fucking. No more fucking!"

        Incontinent three nights
before she died, Jane needed lifting
        onto the commode.
He wiped her and helped her back into bed.
        At five he fed the dog
and returned to find her across the room,
        sitting in a straight chair.
When she couldn't stand, how could she walk?
        He feared she would fall
and called for an ambulance to the hospital
        but when he told Jane,
her mouth twisted down and tears started.

"Do we have to?" He canceled.
Jane said, "Perkins, be with me when I die."
    "Dying is simple," she said.
"What's worst is . . . *the separation.*"
    When she no longer spoke,
they lay alone together, touching,
        and she fixed on him
her beautiful enormous round brown eyes,
        shining, unblinking,
and passionate with love and dread.

        One by one they came,
the oldest and dearest, to say goodbye
        to this friend of the heart.
At first she said their names, wept, and touched;
        then she smiled; then
turned one mouth-corner up. On the last day
        she stared silent goodbyes
with her hands curled and her eyes stuck open.

        Leaving his place beside her,
where her eyes stared, he told her,
        "I'll put these letters
in the box." She had not spoken
        for three hours, and now Jane said
her last words: "O.K."
                        At eight that night,
        her eyes open as they stayed
until she died, brain-stem breathing
        started, he bent to kiss
her pale cool lips again, and felt them
        one last time gather
and purse and peck to kiss him back.

                In the last hours, she kept
    her forearms raised with pale fingers clenched
            at cheek level, like
    the goddess figurine over the bathroom sink.
            Sometimes her right fist flicked
    or spasmed toward her face. For twelve hours
            until she died, he kept
    scratching Jane Kenyon's big bony nose.
            A sharp, almost sweet
    smell began to rise from her open mouth.
            He watched her chest go still.
    With his thumb he closed her round brown eyes.

8

LET IT SPILL

Thelonious Monk

Stephen Dobyns

for Michael Thomas

A record store on Wabash was where
I bought my first album. I was a freshman
in college and played the record in my room

over and over. I was caught by how he took
the musical phrase and seemed to find a new
way out, the next note was never the note

you thought would turn up and yet seemed
correct. Surprise in *'Round Midnight*
or *Sweet and Lovely.* I bought the album

for Mulligan but stayed for Monk. I was
eighteen and between my present and future
was a wall so big that not even sunlight

crossed over. I felt surrounded by all
I couldn't do, as if my hopes to write,
to love, to have children, even to exist

with slight contentment were like ghosts
with the faces found on Japanese masks:
sheer mockery! I would sit on the carpet

and listen to Monk twist the scale into kinks
and curlicues. The gooseneck lamp on my desk
had a blue bulb which I thought artistic and

tinted the stacks of unread books: if Thomas
Mann depressed me, Freud depressed me more.
It seemed that Monk played with sticks attached

to his fingertips as he careened through the tune,
counting unlike any metronome. He was exotic,
his playing was hypnotic. I wish I could say

that hearing him, I grabbed my pack and soldiered
forward. Not quite. It was the surprise I liked,
the discordance and fretful change of beat,

as in *Straight No Chaser*, where he hammers together
a papier-mâché skyscraper, then pops seagulls
with golf balls. Racket, racket, but all of it

music. What Monk banged out was the conviction
of innumerable directions. Years later
I felt he'd been blueprint, map and education:

no streets, we bushwhacked through the underbrush;
not timid, why open your mouth if not to shout?
not scared, the only road lay straight in front;

not polite, the notes themselves were sneak attacks;
not quiet—look, can't you see the sky will soon
collapse and we must keep dancing till it cracks?

The Discovery of Sex

Debra Spencer

We try to be discreet standing in the dark
hallway by the front door. He gets his hands
up inside the front of my shirt and I put mine
down inside the back of his jeans. We are crazy
for skin, each other's skin, warm silky skin.
Our tongues are in each other's mouths,
where they belong, home at last. At first

we hope my mother won't see us, but later we don't care,
we forget her. Suddenly she makes a noise
like a game show alarm and says *Hey! Stop that!*
and we put our hands out where she can see them.
Our mouths stay pressed together, though, and
when she isn't looking anymore our hands go
back inside each other's clothes. We could

go where no one can see us, but we are
good kids, from good families, trying to have
as much discreet sex as possible with my mother and father
four feet away watching strangers kiss on TV,
my mother and father who once did as we are doing,
something we can't imagine because we know

that before we put our mouths together, before
the back seat of his parents' car where our skins
finally become one—before us, these things
were unknown! Our parents look on in disbelief
as we pioneer delights they thought only they knew
before those delights gave them us.

Years later, still we try to be discreet, standing
in the kitchen now where we think she can't see us. I
slip my hands down inside the back of his jeans
and he gets up under the front of my shirt.
We open our mouths to kiss and suddenly *Hey! Hey!*
says our daughter glaring from the kitchen doorway.
Get a room! she says, as we put our hands
out where she can see them.

Lawyer

Carl Sandburg

When the jury files in to deliver a verdict after weeks of direct
      and cross examinations, hot clashes of lawyers and cool
      decisions of the judge,
There are points of high silence—twiddling of thumbs is at an
      end—bailiffs near cuspidors take fresh chews of tobacco
      and wait—and the clock has a chance for its ticking to
      be heard.
A lawyer for the defense clears his throat and holds himself
      ready if the word is "Guilty" to enter motion for a new
      trial, speaking in a soft voice, speaking in a voice slightly
      colored with bitter wrongs mingled with monumental
      patience, speaking with mythic Atlas shoulders of many
      preposterous, unjust circumstances.

The Prodigal Son's Brother

Steve Kowit

who'd been steadfast as small change all his life
forgave the one who bounced back like a bad check
the moment his father told him he ought to.
After all, that's what being good means.
In fact, it was he who hosted the party,
bought the crepes & champagne,
uncorked every bottle. With each drink
another toast to his brother: ex-swindler, hit-man
& rapist. By the end of the night
the entire village was blithering drunk
in an orgy of hugs & forgiveness,
while he himself,
whose one wish was to be loved as profusely,
slipped in & out of their houses,
stuffing into a satchel their brooches & rings
& bracelets & candelabra.
Then lit out at dawn with a light heart
for a port city he knew only by reputation:
ladies in lipstick hanging out of each window,
& every third door a saloon.

Calling Your Father

Robert Bly

There was a boy who never got enough.
You know what I mean. Something
In him longed to find the big
Mother, and he leaped into the sea.

It took a while, but a whale
Agreed to swallow him.
He knew it was wrong, but once
Past the baleen, it was too late.

It's OK. There's a curved library
Inside, and those high
Ladders. People take requests.
It's like the British Museum.

But one has to build a fire.
Maybe it was the romance
Novels he burned. Smoke curls
Up the gorge. She coughs.

And that's it. The boy swims to shore;
It's a fishing town in Alaska.
He finds a telephone booth,
And calls his father. "Let's talk."

Al and Beth

Louis Simpson

My Uncle Al worked in a drugstore
three blocks above Times Square,
dispensing pills and cosmetics.
All day long crazy people
and thieves came into the store,
but nothing seemed to faze him.

His sister, Beth, was the opposite . . .
romantic. She used to sing
on ships that sailed from New York
to Central and South America.
When the tourists came trailing back
on board with their maracas,
Beth would be in the Aztec Room
singing "Smoke Gets in Your Eyes"
and "I Get a Kick out of You."

Once when I argued with Al
about something that America
was doing . . . "My country
right or wrong," he told me.
I suppose so, if you've come
from a village in Russia no one
ever heard of, with no drains,
and on saints' days the Cossacks
descend on you with the blessing
of the Church, to beat out your brains.

And when, after a fortnight
being seasick, there's the statue,
and buildings reaching up
to the sky. Streets full of people.
The clang of a bell, someone yelling
as you almost get run over.
More things happening every second
in New York, than Lutsk in a year.

Al lived on Kingston Avenue, Brooklyn,
all of his life, with the wife
his mother had picked out for him.
Beth never married. She was still waiting
for Mr. Right.

              Of such is the Kingdom
of Heaven. Say that I sent you.

The Meeting

Henry Wadsworth Longfellow

After so long an absence
　　At last we meet again:
Does the meeting give us pleasure,
　　Or does it give us pain?

The tree of life has been shaken,
　　And but few of us linger now,
Like the Prophet's two or three berries
　　In the top of the uppermost bough.

We cordially greet each other
　　In the old, familiar tone;
And we think, though we do not say it,
　　How old and gray he is grown!

We speak of a Merry Christmas
　　And many a Happy New Year;
But each in his heart is thinking
　　Of those that are not here.

We speak of friends and their fortunes,
　　And of what they did and said,
Till the dead alone seem living,
　　And the living alone seem dead.

And at last we hardly distinguish
    Between the ghosts and the guests;
And a mist and shadow of sadness
    Steals over our merriest jests.

Nothing Is Lost

Noël Coward

Deep in our sub-conscious, we are told
Lie all our memories, lie all the notes
Of all the music we have ever heard
And all the phrases those we loved have spoken,
Sorrows and losses time has since consoled,
Family jokes, out-moded anecdotes
Each sentimental souvenir and token
Everything seen, experienced, each word
Addressed to us in infancy, before
Before we could even know or understand
The implications of our wonderland.
There they all are, the legendary lies
The birthday treats, the sights, the sounds, the tears
Forgotten debris of forgotten years
Waiting to be recalled, waiting to rise
Before our world dissolves before our eyes
Waiting for some small, intimate reminder,
A word, a tune, a known familiar scent
An echo from the past when, innocent
We looked upon the present with delight
And doubted not the future would be kinder
And never knew the loneliness of night.

The Planet on the Table

Wallace Stevens

Ariel was glad he had written his poems.
They were of a remembered time
Or of something seen that he liked.

Other makings of the sun
Were waste and welter
And the ripe shrub writhed.

His self and the sun were one
And his poems, although makings of his self,
Were no less makings of the sun.

It was not important that they survive.
What mattered was that they should bear
Some lineament or character,

Some affluence, if only half-perceived,
In the poverty of their words,
Of the planet of which they were part.

It Is Raining on the
House of Anne Frank

Linda Pastan

It is raining on the house
of Anne Frank
and on the tourists
herded together under the shadow
of their umbrellas,
on the perfectly silent
tourists who would rather be
somewhere else
but who wait here on stairs
so steep they must rise
to some occasion
high in the empty loft,
in the quaint toilet,
in the skeleton
of a kitchen
or on the map—
each of its arrows
a barb of wire—
with all the dates, the expulsions,
the forbidding shapes
of continents.
And across Amsterdam it is raining
on the Van Gogh Museum
where we will hurry next

to see how someone else
could find the pure
center of light
within the dark circle
of his demons.

The Sunlight on the Garden

Louis MacNeice

The sunlight on the garden
Hardens and grows cold,
We cannot cage the minute
Within its nets of gold,
When all is told
We cannot beg for pardon.

Our freedom as free lances
Advances towards its end;
The earth compels, upon it
Sonnets and birds descend;
And soon, my friend,
We shall have no time for dances.

The sky was good for flying
Defying the church bells
And every evil iron
Siren and what it tells:
The earth compels,
We are dying, Egypt, dying

And not expecting pardon,
Hardened in heart anew,
But glad to have sat under
Thunder and rain with you,
And grateful too
For sunlight on the garden.

too sweet

Charles Bukowski

I have been going to the track for so
long that
all the employees know
me,
and now with winter here
it's dark before the last
race.
as I walk to the parking lot
the valet recognizes my
slouching gait
and before I reach him
my car is waiting for me,
lights on, engine warm.
the other patrons
(still waiting)
ask,
"who the hell is that
guy?"

I slip the valet a
tip, the size depending upon the
luck of the
day (and my luck has been amazingly
good lately)
and I then am in the machine and out on
the street

as the horses break
from the gate.

I drive east down Century Blvd.
turning on the radio to get the result of that
last race.

at first the announcer is concerned only with
bad weather and poor freeway
conditions.
we are old friends: I have listened to his
voice for decades but,
of course, the time will finally come
when neither one of us will need to
clip our toenails or
heed the complaints of our
women any longer.

meanwhile, there is a certain rhythm
to the essentials that now need
attending to.
I light my cigarette
check the dashboard
adjust the seat and
weave between a Volks and a Fiat.
as flecks of rain spatter the
windshield
I decide not to die just
yet:
this good life just smells too
sweet.

For My Sister, Emigrating

Wendy Cope

You've left with me
the things you couldn't take
or bear to give away—
books, records and a biscuit-tin
that Nanna gave you.

It's old and dirty
and the lid won't fit.
Standing in a corner of my room,
quite useless, it's as touching
as a once loved toy.

Yes, sentimental now—
but if you'd stayed,
we would have quarrelled
just the same as ever,
found excuses not to phone.

We never learn. We've grown up
struggling, frightened
that the family would drown us,
only giving in to love
when someone's dead or gone.

The Three Kings

Muriel Spark

Where do we go from here?
We left our country,
Bore gifts,
Followed a star.
We were questioned.
We answered.
We reached our objective.
We enjoyed the trip.
Then we came back by a different way.
And now the people are demonstrating in the streets.
They say they don't need the Kings any more.
They did very well in our absence.
Everything was all right without us.
They are out on the streets with placards:
Wise Men? What's wise about them?
There are plenty of Wise Men,
And who needs them?—and so on.

Perhaps they will be better off without us,
But where do we go from here?

Not Only the Eskimos

Lisel Mueller

We have only one noun
but as many different kinds:

the grainy snow of the Puritans
and snow of soft, fat flakes,

guerrilla snow, which comes in the night
and changes the world by morning,

rabbinical snow, a permanent skullcap
on the highest mountains,

snow that blows in like the Lone Ranger,
riding hard from out of the West,

surreal snow in the Dakotas,
when you can't find your house, your street,
though you are not in a dream
or a science-fiction movie,

snow that tastes good to the sun
when it licks black tree limbs,
leaving us only one white stripe,
a replica of a skunk,

unbelievable snows:
the blizzard that strikes on the tenth of April,
the false snow before Indian summer,
the Big Snow on Mozart's birthday,
when Chicago became the Elysian fields
and strangers spoke to each other,

paper snow, cut and taped
to the inside of grade-school windows,

in an old tale, the snow
that covers a nest of strawberries,
small hearts, ripe and sweet,

the special snow that goes with Christmas,
whether it falls or not,

the Russian snow we remember
along with the warmth and smell of our furs,
though we have never traveled
to Russia or worn furs,

Villon's snows of yesteryear,
lost with ladies gone out like matches,
the snow in Joyce's "The Dead,"
the silent, secret snow
in a story by Conrad Aiken,
which is the snow of first love,

the snowfall between the child
and the spacewoman on TV,

snow as idea of whiteness,
as in *snowdrop, snow goose, snowball bush,*

the snow that puts stars in your hair,
and your hair, which has turned to snow,

the snow Elinor Wylie walked in
in velvet shoes,

the snow before her footprints
and the snow after,

the snow in the back of our heads,
whiter than white, which has to do
with childhood again each year.

Where Go the Boats

Robert Louis Stevenson

Dark brown is the river,
    Golden is the sand.
It flows along for ever,
    With trees on either hand.

Green leaves a-floating,
    Castles of the foam,
Boats of mine a-boating—
    Where will all come home?

On goes the river
    And out past the mill,
Away down the valley,
    Away down the hill.

Away down the river,
    A hundred miles or more,
Other little children
    Shall bring my boats ashore.

The Parade

Billy Collins

How exhilarating it was to march
along the great boulevards
in the sunflash of trumpets
and under all the waving flags—
the flag of desire, the flag of ambition.

So many of us streaming along—
all of humanity, really—
moving in perfect sync,
yet each lost in the room of a private dream.

How stimulating the scenery of the world,
the rows of roadside trees,
the huge blue sheet of the sky.

How endless it seemed until we veered
off the broad turnpike
into a pasture of high grass,
heading toward the dizzying cliffs of mortality.

Generation after generation,
we shoulder forward
under the play of clouds
until we high-step off the sharp lip into space.

So I should not have to remind you
that little time is given here
to rest on a wayside bench,
to stop and bend to the wildflowers,
or to study a bird on a branch—

not when the young
keep shoving from behind,
not when the old are tugging us forward,
pulling on our arms with all their feeble strength.

My Cup

Robert Friend

They tell me I am going to die.
Why don't I seem to care?
My cup is full. Let it spill.

Affirmation

Donald Hall

To grow old is to lose everything.
Aging, everybody knows it.
Even when we are young,
we glimpse it sometimes, and nod our heads
when a grandfather dies.
Then we row for years on the midsummer
pond, ignorant and content. But a marriage,
that began without harm, scatters
into debris on the shore,
and a friend from school drops
cold on a rocky strand.
If a new love carries us
past middle age, our wife will die
at her strongest and most beautiful.
New women come and go. All go.
The pretty lover who announces
that she is temporary
is temporary. The bold woman,
middle-aged against our old age,
sinks under an anxiety she cannot withstand.
Another friend of decades estranges himself
in words that pollute thirty years.
Let us stifle under mud at the pond's edge
and affirm that it is fitting
and delicious to lose everything.

A Singing Voice

Kenneth Rexroth

Once, camping on a high bluff
Above the Fox River, when
I was about fourteen years
Old, on a full moonlit night
Crowded with whippoorwills and
Frogs, I lay awake long past
Midnight watching the moon move
Through the half drowned stars. Suddenly
I heard, far away on the warm
Air a high clear soprano,
Purer than the purest boy's
Voice, singing, "Tuck me to sleep
In my old 'Tucky home."
She was in an open car
Speeding along the winding
Dipping highway beneath me.
A few seconds later
An old touring car full of
Boys and girls rushed by under
Me, the soprano rising
Full and clear and now close by
I could hear the others singing
Softly behind her voice. Then
Rising and falling with the
Twisting road the song closed, soft
In the night. Over thirty

Years have gone by but I have
Never forgotten. Again
And again, driving on a
Lonely moonlit road, or waking
In a warm murmurous night,
I hear that voice singing that
Common song like an
Angelic memory.

Since You Asked

Lawrence Raab

for a friend who asked
to be in a poem

Since you asked, let's make it dinner
at your house—a celebration
for no reason, which is always
the best occasion. Are you worried
there won't be enough space, enough food?

But in a poem we can do anything we want.
Look how easy it is to add on rooms, to multiply
the wine and chickens. And while we're at it
let's take those trees that died last winter
and bring them back to life.

Things should look pulled together,
and we could use the shade—so even now
they shudder and unfold their bright new leaves.
And now the guests are arriving—everyone
you expected, then others as well:

friends who never became your friends,
the women you didn't marry, all their children.
And the dead—I didn't tell you
but they're always included in these gatherings—
hesitant and shy, they hang back at first

among the blossoming trees.
You have only to say their names,
ask them inside. Everyone will find a place
at your table. What more can I do?
The glasses are filled, the children are quiet.

My friend, it must be time for you to speak.

Inviting a Friend to Supper

Ben Jonson

To-night, grave sir, both my poore house, and I
Doe equally desire your companie:
Not that we thinke us worthy such a guest,
But that your worth will dignifie our feast,
With those that come; whose grace may make that seeme

Something, which, else, could hope for no esteeme.
It is the faire acceptance, Sir, creates
The entertaynment perfect: not the cates.
Yet shall you have, to rectifie your palate,
An olive, capers, or some better sallad
Ushring the mutton; with a short-leg'd hen,
If we can get her, full of eggs, and then,
Limons, and wine for sauce: to these, a coney
Is not to be despair'd of, for our money;
And, though fowle, now, be scarce, yet there are clerkes,
The skie not falling, thinke we may have larkes.
I'll tell you of more, and lye, so you will come:
Of partrich, pheasant, wood-cock, of which some
May yet be there; and godwit, if we can:
Knat, raile, and ruffe too. How so e'er, my man
Shall reade a piece of VIRGIL, TACITUS,
LIVIE, or of some better booke to us,
Of which wee'll speake our minds, amidst our meate;
And I'll professe no verses to repeate:
To this, if ought appeare, which I know not of,

That will the pastrie, not my paper, show of.
Digestive cheese, and fruit there sure will bee;
But that, which most doth take my *Muse*, and mee,
Is a pure cup of rich *Canary*-wine,
Which is the *Mermaids*, now, but shall be mine:
Of which had HORACE, or ANACREON tasted,
Their lives, as doe their lines, till now had lasted.
Tabacco, Nectar, or the *Thespian* spring,
Are all but LUTHERS beere, to this I sing.
Of this we will sup free, but moderately,
And we will have no *Pooly,* or *Parrot* by;
Nor shall our cups make any guiltie men:
But, at our parting, we will be, as when
We innocently met. No simple word
That shall be utter'd at our mirthfull board
Shall make us sad next morning: or affright
The libertie, that wee'll enjoy to-night.

The Love Cook

Ron Padgett

Let me cook you some dinner.
Sit down and take off your shoes
and socks and in fact the rest
of your clothes, have a daiquiri,
turn on some music and dance
around the house, inside and out,
it's night and the neighbors
are sleeping, those dolts, and
the stars are shining bright,
and I've got the burners lit
for you, you hungry thing.

Soda Crackers

Raymond Carver

You soda crackers! I remember
when I arrived here in the rain,
whipped out and alone.
How we shared the aloneness
and quiet of this house.
And the doubt that held me
from fingers to toes
as I took you out
of your cellophane wrapping
and ate you, meditatively,
at the kitchen table
that first night with cheese,
and mushroom soup. Now,
a month later to the day,
an important part of us
is still here. I'm fine.
And you—I'm proud of you, too.
You're even getting remarked
on in print! Every soda cracker
should be so lucky.
We've done all right for
ourselves. Listen to me.
I never thought
I could go on like this

about soda crackers.
But I tell you
the clear sunshiny
days are here, at last.

That Silent Evening

Galway Kinnell

I will go back to that silent evening
when we lay together and talked in low, silent voices,
while outside slow lumps of soft snow
fell, hushing as they got near the ground,
with a fire in the room, in which centuries
of tree went up in continuous ghost-giving-up,
without a crackle, into morning light.
Not until what hastens went slower did we sleep.
When we got home we turned and looked back
at our tracks twining out of the woods,
where the branches we brushed against let fall
puffs of sparkling snow, quickly, in silence,
like stolen kisses, and where the *scritch scritch scritch*
among the trees, which is the sound that dies
inside the sparks from the wedge when the sledge
hits it off center telling everything inside
it is fire, jumped to a black branch, puffed up
but without arms and so to our eyes lonesome,
and yet also—how could we know this?—*happy!*
in shape of chickadee. Lying still in snow,
not iron-willed, like railroad tracks, willing
not to meet until heaven, but here and there
making slubby kissing stops in the field,
our tracks wobble across the snow their long scratch.
Everything that happens here is really little more,
if even that, than a scratch, too. Words, in our mouths,

are almost ready, already, to bandage the one
whom the *scritch scritch scritch,* meaning *if how when*
we might lose each other, scratches scratches scratches
from this moment to that. Then I will go back
to that silent evening, when the past just managed
to overlap the future, if only by a trace,
and the light doubles and shines
through the dark the sparkling that heavens the earth.

This Is How Memory Works

Patricia Hampl

You are stepping off a train.
A wet blank night, the smell of cinders.
A gust of steam from the engine swirls
around the hem of your topcoat, around
the hand holding the brown leather valise,
the hand that, a moment ago, slicked back
the hair and then put on the fedora
in front of the mirror with the beveled
edges in the cherrywood compartment.

The girl standing on the platform
in the Forties dress
has curled her hair, she has
nylon stockings—no, silk stockings still.
Her shoulders are touchingly military,
squared by those shoulder pads
and a sweet faith in the Allies.
She is waiting for you.
She can be wearing a hat, if you like.

You see her first.
That's part of the beauty:
you get the pure, eager face,
the lyrical dress, the surprise.
You can have the steam,
the crowded depot, the camel's-hair coat,
real leather and brass clasps on the suitcase;
you can make the lights glow with
strange significance, and the black cars
that pass you are historical yet ordinary.

The girl is yours,
the flowery dress, the walk
to the streetcar, a fried egg sandwich
and a joke about Mussolini.
You can have it all:
you're in *that* world, the only way
you'll ever be there now, hired
for your silent hammer, to nail pictures
to the walls of this mansion
made of thinnest air.

"The Purpose of Time Is to Prevent Everything from Happening at Once"

X. J. Kennedy

Suppose your life a folded telescope
Durationless, collapsed in just a flash
As from your mother's womb you, bawling, drop
Into a nursing home. Suppose you crash
Your car, your marriage—toddler laying waste
A field of daisies, schoolkid, zit-faced teen
With lover zipping up your pants in haste
Hearing your parents' tread downstairs—all one.

Einstein was right. That would be too intense.
You need a chance to preen, to give a dull
Recital before an indifferent audience
Equally slow in jeering you and clapping.
Time takes its time unraveling. But, still,
You'll wonder when your life ends: Huh? What happened?

9

I FEEL OUR KINSHIP

Death Mask

Edward Field

"Old age is the most unexpected
of all the things that happen to a man."
—LEON TROTSKY

"Do not let me hear
Of the wisdom of old men, but rather of their folly,
Their fear . . ."
—"EAST COKER," BY T. S. ELIOT

1

In the mirror now,
    what I see
reminds me
    I won't be here forever.

I don't feel like
    that face at all.
Inside it, I protest,
    I'm quite different.

It's somebody's grandfather,
    not me.

Whose grandfather is that?
    I don't want him.

2

Ah, memory, memory . . .

terrible,

to be losing

the words.

3

How do you get from here to there—
I mean, from where I am
to the nursing home?
In a snap of the fingers,
the blink of an eye.

Like my mother said,
as she was being loaded
into the ambulance,
It went so fast.

4

Life
        a lazy buzz,
then
        the quick sting.

A long inward breath,
    then
the sudden
    exhaling.

That's the Sum of It

David Ignatow

I don't know which to mourn. Both have died on me, my wife and
my car. I feel strongly about my car, but I am also affected by my
wife. Without my car, I can't leave the house to keep myself from
being alone. My wife gave me two children, both of whom, of
course,
no longer live with us, as was to be expected, as we in our youth
left
our parents behind. With my car, I could visit my children, when
they
are not too busy.

Before she died, my wife urged me to find another woman. It's
advice
I'd like to take up but not without a car. Without a car, I cannot
find
myself another woman. That's the sum of it.

Suck It Up

Paul Zimmer

Two pugs on the undercard step through
The ropes in satin robes,
Pink Adidas with tassels,
Winking at the women in the crowd.
At instructions they stare down hard
And refuse to touch their gloves,
Trying to make everyone believe
That this will be a serious dust-up.

But when the bell rings they start
Slapping like a couple of Barbie Dolls.
One throws a half-hearted hook,
The other flicks out his jab,
They bounce around for a while
Then grab each other for a tango.
The crowd gets tired of booing
and half of them go out for a beer,
But I've got no place to hide.

A week after a cancer scare,
A year from a detached retina,
Asthmatic, overweight, trickling,
Drooling, bent like a blighted elm
In my pajamas and slippers,
I have tuned up my hearing aids to sit in
Numbness without expectation before
These televised Tuesday Night Fights.

With a minute left in the fourth,
Scuffling, they butt their heads
By accident. In midst of all the catcalls
And hubbub suddenly they realize
How much they hate each other.

They start hammering and growling,
Really dealing, whistling combinations,
Hitting on the breaks and thumbing.
At least one guy crosses a stiff jab
With a roundhouse right and the other
Loses his starch. The guy wades into
The wounded one, pounding him
Back and forth until he goes down,
Bouncing his head hard on the canvas.

The count begins but he is saved
By the bell and his trainers haul
Him to his stool as the lens zooms in.

I come to the edge of my La-Z-Boy,
Blinking and groaning from my incision,
Eager for wise, insightful instruction.

He gets a bucket of water in his face,
A sniff on the salts while the cutman
Tries to close his wounds with glue.
His nose is broken, eyes are crossed,
His lips bleed like two rare steaks.
His cornermen take turns slapping his cheeks.
"Suck it up!" they shout.
"Suck it up!"

The Day the Tree Fell Down

Jack LaZebnik

crumbling. It died of old age,
I tell you, like a man. We wept.
We had worn our time upon it, put
our arms around to touch fingertips
and we measured ourselves, our feelings
on the years. We made our calculations
pay, then. Now, the fears, age,
daily mathematics. The tree held
the green. Birds, squirrels, coons
made memory there until the day it fell.
They got out. It groaned for twenty minutes.
I tell you, it sighed as it bent,
its branches catching the dull fall,
the soft turning in wet dissolution.
The body lay exposed: a gut of grubs,
a lust of hollowness. We wept,
as I say, more than it was called for.

White Autumn

Robert Morgan

She had always loved to read, even
in childhood during the Confederate War,
and built the habit later of staying up
by the oil lamp near the fireplace after
husband and children slept, the scrub-work done.
She fed the addiction in the hard years
of Reconstruction and even after
her husband died and she was forced
to provide and be sole foreman of the place.
While her only son fought in France
it was this second life, by the open window
in warm months when the pines on the hill
seemed to talk to the creek, or katydids
lined-out their hymns in the trees beyond the barn,
or by the familiar of fire in winter,
that sustained her. She and her daughters
later forgot the time, the exact date,
if there was such a day, she made her decision.
But after the children could cook
and garden and milk and bring in a little
by housecleaning for the rich in Flat Rock,
and the son returned from overseas
wounded but still able and married a war widow,
and when she had found just the right chair,
a rocker joined by a man over on Willow
from rubbed hickory, with cane seat and back,

and arms wide enough to rest her everlasting cup
of coffee on, or a heavy book,
she knew she had come to her place and would stay.
And from that day, if it was one time and not
a gradual recognition, she never crossed a threshold
or ventured from that special seat of rightness,
of presence and pleasure, except to be helped to bed
in the hours before dawn for a little nap.
That chair—every Christmas someone gave her a bright
cushion to break in—was the site on which she bathed
in a warm river of books and black coffee,
varieties of candy and cakes kept in a low cupboard
at hand. The cats passed through her lap and legs
and through the rungs of her seat. The tons
of firewood came in cold and left as light, smoke, ash.
She rode that upright cradle to sleep
and through many long visits with tiers of family,
kissing the babies like different kinds of fruit.
Always hiding the clay pipe in her cabinet
when company appeared. She chaired decisions
to keep the land and refused welfare.
On that creaking throne she ruled a tiny kingdom
through war, death of kin. Even on the night she did
stop breathing, near a hundred, no one knew
exactly when, but found the lamp still on,
the romance open to a new chapter,
and the sun just appearing at her elbow.

Naked

Jennifer Michael Hecht

The reason you so often in literature have a naked woman
walk out of her house that way, usually older, in her front garden
or on the sidewalk, oblivious, is because of exactly how I feel right
   now.

You tend to hear about how it felt to come upon such a mythical
   beast,
the naked woman on the street, the naked man in a tree, and that
   makes
sense because it is wonderful to take the naked woman by the
   hand

And know that you will remember that moment for the rest of
   your life
because of what it means, the desperation, the cataclysm of what
   it takes
to leave your house naked or to take off your clothes in the tree.

It feels good to get the naked man to come down from there by a
   series
of gentle commands and take him by the elbow or her by the hand
   and
lead him to his home like you would care for a bird or a human
   heart.

Still if you want instead, for once, to hear about how the person
    came to be
standing there, naked, outside, you should talk to me right now,
    quickly,
before I forget the details of this way that I feel. I feel like walking
    out.

Slow Children at Play

Cecilia Woloch

All the quick children have gone inside, called
by their mothers to *hurry-up-wash-your-hands*
honey-dinner's-getting-cold, just-wait-till-your-father-gets-home—
and only the slow children out on the lawns, marking off
paths between fireflies, making soft little sounds with their
    mouths, *ohs*
that glow and go out and glow. And their slow mothers
    flickering,
pale in the dusk, watching them turn in the gentle air, watching
    them
twirling, their arms spread wide, thinking, *These are my children,*
    thinking,
Where is their dinner? Where has their father gone?

Driving to Town Late to Mail a Letter

Robert Bly

It is a cold and snowy night. The main street is deserted.
The only things moving are swirls of snow.
As I lift the mailbox door, I feel its cold iron.
There is a privacy I love in this snowy night.
Driving around, I will waste more time.

My brother's in Wyoming . . .

Gary Young

My brother's in Wyoming, and I've had that dream again. We're fishing. The trout rise, take our bait, and keep rising. In love once with a woman, and with my own capacity for pain, I fell in with some cowboys, and broke my neck riding bulls in a little rodeo. That night, drunk in the bunkhouse, not knowing how badly I'd been hurt, I thought it can't get worse than this, but I was wrong. That was twenty years ago. Thunder rolls down South Fork Canyon. The Milky Way is a great river overhead. My brother is in Wyoming. I miss him more than ever when he's there.

My Brother

Denver Butson

To escape headaches and fears of an unfaithful wife
my brother   perpetually reforming drug user
machinist   scrapper   arrested at 14 for arson
and incarcerated for a few weeks
father of one son and one aborted fetus
occasional bowler   heavy metal fan
connoisseur of ketchup   potato chips   stromboli
and cheesesteak   wearer of faded jeans
faded flannel shirts   pocket-tee shirts
unlaced hightops or workboots
concert tee shirts   painters' hats and
army coat   sufferer of aloneness
of paranoia and fear   insomniac and talker
of another language in his sleep
expert belcher and marksman   constant but lousy liar
moderate drinker of cheap beer   violent rampager
demolisher of lamps   electric fans   telephones
blue-eyed ladies' man   father   brother   and son
shy blushing ladies' man   skinny-legged blue-eyed
ladies' man   stuck the open end of a .357 Magnum
in his right nostril with the other end
in his calloused and stained hands
and blew his headaches and his head
from this world into the next
one night   just like that.

Still Life

Carl Sandburg

Cool your heels on the rail of an observation car.
Let the engineer open her up for ninety miles an hour.
Take in the prairie right and left, rolling land and new hay crops,
     swaths of new hay laid in the sun.
A gray village flecks by and the horses hitched in front of the
     post office never blink an eye.
A barnyard and fifteen Holstein cows, dabs of white on a black
     wall map, never blink an eye.
A signalman in a tower, the outpost of Kansas City, keeps his
     place at a window with the serenity of a bronze statue on
     a dark night when lovers pass whispering.

The Changing Light

Lawrence Ferlinghetti

The changing light
        at San Francisco
     is none of your East Coast light
      none of your
          pearly light of Paris
The light of San Francisco
       is a sea light
           an island
light
And the light of fog
         blanketing the hills
       drifting in at night
        through the Golden Gate
          to lie on
the city at dawn
And then the halcyon late mornings
        after the fog burns off
         and the sun paints white houses
          with the sea
light of Greece
        with sharp clean shadows
          making the town look like
         it had just been
painted

But the wind comes up at four o'clock
                    sweeping the
hills

 And then the veil of light of early evening

And then another scrim
                    when the new night fog
                    floats in
And in that vale of light
                    the city drifts
                                anchorless
upon the ocean

At the Fishhouses

Elizabeth Bishop

Although it is a cold evening,
down by one of the fishhouses
an old man sits netting,
his net, in the gloaming almost invisible,
a dark purple-brown,
and his shuttle worn and polished.
The air smells so strong of codfish
it makes one's nose run and one's eyes water.
The five fishhouses have steeply peaked roofs
and narrow, cleated gangplanks slant up
to storerooms in the gables
for the wheelbarrows to be pushed up and down on.
All is silver: the heavy surface of the sea,
swelling slowly as if considering spilling over,
is opaque, but the silver of the benches,
the lobster pots, and masts, scattered
among the wild jagged rocks,
is of an apparent translucence
like the small old buildings with an emerald moss
growing on their shoreward walls.
The big fish tubs are completely lined
with layers of beautiful herring scales
and the wheelbarrows are similarly plastered
with creamy iridescent coats of mail,
with small iridescent flies crawling on them.
Up on the little slope behind the houses,

set in the sparse bright sprinkle of grass,
is an ancient wooden capstan,
cracked, with two long bleached handles
and some melancholy stains, like dried blood,
where the ironwork has rusted.
The old man accepts a Lucky Strike.
He was a friend of my grandfather.
We talk of the decline in the population
and of codfish and herring
while he waits for a herring boat to come in.
There are sequins on his vest and on his thumb.
He has scraped the scales, the principal beauty,
from unnumbered fish with that black old knife,
the blade of which is almost worn away.

Down at the water's edge, at the place
where they haul up the boats, up the long ramp
descending into the water, thin silver
tree trunks are laid horizontally
across the gray stones, down and down
at intervals of four or five feet.

Cold dark deep and absolutely clear,
element bearable to no mortal,
to fish and to seals . . . One seal particularly
I have seen here evening after evening.
He was curious about me. He was interested in music;
like me a believer in total immersion,
so I used to sing him Baptist hymns.
I also sang "A Mighty Fortress Is Our God."
He stood up in the water and regarded me
steadily, moving his head a little.
Then he would disappear, then suddenly emerge
almost in the same spot, with a sort of shrug

as if it were against his better judgment.
Cold dark deep and absolutely clear,
the clear gray icy water . . . Back, behind us,
the dignified tall firs begin.
Bluish, associating with their shadows,
a million Christmas trees stand
waiting for Christmas. The water seems suspended
above the rounded gray and blue-gray stones.
I have seen it over and over, the same sea, the same,
slightly, indifferently swinging above the stones,
icily free above the stones,
above the stones and then the world.
If you should dip your hand in,
your wrist would ache immediately,
your bones would begin to ache and your hand would burn
as if the water were a transmutation of fire
that feeds on stones and burns with a dark gray flame.
If you tasted it, it would first taste bitter,
then briny, then surely burn your tongue.
It is like what we imagine knowledge to be:
dark, salt, clear, moving, utterly free,
drawn from the cold hard mouth
of the world, derived from the rocky breasts
forever, flowing and drawn, and since
our knowledge is historical, flowing, and flown.

A Man In Maine

Philip Booth

North. The bare time.
The same quick dark
from Rutland to Nome,

the utter chill.
Winter stars. After
work, splitting birch

by the light outside
his back door, a man
in Maine thinks what

his father told him,
splitting outside
this same back door:

every November, his
father said, he thought
when he split wood

of what his father
said the night he
right here died: just

after supper, his
father said, his father
came out back, looked

out at the sky
the way he had
for years, picked up

his ax, struck
the oak clean, and
was himself struck

down; before he
died he just had
this to say:

this time of
year the stars
come close some fierce.

The War in the Air

Howard Nemerov

For a saving grace, we didn't see our dead,
Who rarely bothered coming home to die
But simply stayed away out there
In the clean war, the war in the air.

Seldom the ghosts came back bearing their tales
Of hitting the earth, the incompressible sea,

But stayed up there in the relative wind,
Shades fading in the mind,

Who had no graves but only epitaphs
Where never so many spoke for never so few:
Per ardua, said the partisans of Mars,
Per aspera, to the stars.

That was the good war, the war we won
As if there were no death, for goodness' sake,
With the help of the losers we left out there
In the air, in the empty air.

In the Middle

Barbara Crooker

of a life that's as complicated as everyone else's,
struggling for balance, juggling time.
The mantle clock that was my grandfather's
has stopped at 9:20; we haven't had time
to get it repaired. The brass pendulum is still,
the chimes don't ring. One day you look out the window,
green summer, the next, and the leaves have already fallen,
and a grey sky lowers the horizon. Our children almost grown,
our parents gone, it happened so fast. Each day, we must learn
again how to love, between morning's quick coffee
and evening's slow return. Steam from a pot of soup rises,
mixing with the yeasty smell of baking bread. Our bodies
twine, and the big black dog pushes his great head between;
his tail is a metronome, 3/4 time. We'll never get there,
Time is always ahead of us, running down the beach, urging
us on faster, faster, but sometimes we take off our watches,
sometimes we lie in the hammock, caught between the mesh
of rope and the net of stars, suspended, tangled up
in love, running out of time.

Are You Tired of Me, My Darling?

Traditional

Are you tired of me, my darling?
Did you mean those words you said
That made me love you forever
Since the day when we were wed—
I still recall the springtime
When the two of us first met
And spoke words of warm affection,
Words my heart can ne'er forget.

Do you think the bloom's departed
From the cheeks you once thought fair?
Do you think I've grown cold-hearted
From a load of toil and care?
Tell me, would you do it over?
Or would you make it otherwise?
Are you tired of me, my darling?
Answer only with your eyes.

On a Night of Snow

Elizabeth Coatsworth

Cat, if you go outdoors, you must walk in the snow.
You will come back with little white shoes on your feet,
little white shoes of snow that have heels of sleet.
Stay by the fire, my Cat. Lie still, do not go.
See how the flames are leaping and hissing low,
I will bring you a saucer of milk like a marguerite,
so white and so smooth, so spherical and so sweet—
stay with me, Cat. Outdoors the wild winds blow.

Outdoors the wild winds blow, Mistress, and dark is the night,
strange voices cry in the trees, intoning strange lore,
and more than cats move, lit by our eyes' green light,
on silent feet where the meadow grasses hang hoar—
Mistress, there are portents abroad of magic and might,
and things that are yet to be done. Open the door!

Closing in on the Harvest

Leo Dangel

No one could stop him.
A bad heart, he still
worked in the field
and said he would die
on the tractor.
Out on the Super-M
picking corn, somehow
he got off, though,
and sat on the ground,
leaning against the tire,
where we found him.
His eyes were wide open,
looking mean as hell,
like when he was alive
and chores weren't done,
but his hand
lay on his chest, gentle,
making us think
he was pledging something.
We could smell
the dry wind.
The tractor radio was on
to the World Series—
Cardinals 7, Yankees 5,

Bob Gibson on the mound,
one out to go—
the steel corn wagon
was not quite full.

Reconciliation

Walt Whitman

Word over all, beautiful as the sky,
Beautiful that war and all its deeds of carnage must in time be
    utterly lost,
That the hands of the sisters Death and Night incessantly
    softly wash again, and ever again, this soil'd world;
For my enemy is dead, a man divine as myself is dead,
I look where he lies white-faced and still in the coffin—I draw
    near,
Bend down and touch lightly with my lips the white face in
    the coffin.

Tie the Strings to my Life, My Lord

Emily Dickinson

Tie the Strings to my Life, My Lord,
Then, I am ready to go!
Just a look at the Horses—
Rapid! That will do!

Put me in on the firmest side—
So I shall never fall—
For we must ride to the Judgment—
And it's partly, down Hill—

But never I mind the steepest—
And never I mind the Sea—
Held fast in Everlasting Race—
By my own Choice, and Thee—

Goodbye to the Life I used to live—
And the World I used to know—
And kiss the Hills, for me, just once—
Then—I am ready to go!

The Last Waltz

Alden Nowlan

The orchestra playing
the last waltz
at three o'clock
in the morning
in the Knights of Pythias Hall
in Hartland, New Brunswick,
Canada, North America,
world, solar system,
centre of the universe—

and all of us drunk,
swaying together
to the music of rum
and a sad clarinet:

comrades all,
each with his beloved.

Rye Whiskey

Traditional

I'll eat when I'm hungry, I'll drink when I'm dry,
If hard times don't kill me, I'll live till I die.
O whiskey, you villain, you've been my downfall.
You've beat me, you've banged me, but I love you for all.

Jack o' Diamonds, Jack o' Diamonds, I know you of old.
You've robbed my poor pockets of silver and gold.
I'll drink and I'll gamble, my money's my own,
And them that don't like it can leave me alone.

My boot's in the stirrup, my bridle's in hand,
I'm leaving sweet Molly, the fairest in the land.
Her parents don't like me, they say I'm too poor.
They say I'm unworthy to enter her door.

You boast of your knowledge and brag of your sense
But it'll all be forgotten a hundred years hence.
Rye whiskey, rye whiskey, rye whiskey I cry,
If I don't get rye whiskey I surely will die.

Let Old Nellie Stay

Traditional

It was late in the evening,
The guests were all leaving,
O'Malley was closing the bar.
He turned and he said
To the old lady in red,
 "Get up! You can't stay where you are."

She shed a big tear
In her bucket of beer,
Tears flowed from her eyes so red.
When a bull rider dapper
Stepped out of the crapper,
And these are the words that he said:

"Her mother never told her
The things a young girl should know,
About these traveling bull riders
And the way they come and go.
So do not treat her harshly
Because she went too far,
But be a little kindhearted
And let old Nellie sleep under the bar."

In Praise of My Bed

Meredith Holmes

At last I can be with you!
The grinding hours
since I left your side!
The labor of being fully human,
working my opposable thumb,
talking, and walking upright.
Now I have unclasped
unzipped, stepped out of.
Husked, soft, a be-er only,
I do nothing, but point
my bare feet into your
clean smoothness
feel your quiet strength
the whole length of my body.
I close my eyes, hear myself
moan, so grateful to be held this way.

Poem for the Family

Susan Cataldo

Before I went to sleep, the soft lamplights
from the tenements across the street,
still, in the night, resembled peace.
There is something I forgot to be grateful
for. But I'm not uneasy. This poem
is enough gratitude for the day. That leaf
tapping against the window, enough
music for the night. My love's even
breathing, a lullaby for me.
Gentle is the sun's touch
as it brushes the earth's revolutions.
Fragrant is the moon in February's
sky. Stars look down & witness,
never judge. The City moves
beneath me, out of sight.
O let this poem be a planet
or a haven. Heaven for a poet
homeward bound. Rest my son's head
upon sweet dreams & contentment.
Let me turn out the light to rest.

In Bed with a Book

Mona Van Duyn

In police procedurals they are dying all over town,
the life ripped out of them, by gun, bumper, knife,
hammer, dope, etcetera, and no clues at all.
All through the book the calls come in: body found
in bed, car, street, lake, park, garage, library,
and someone goes out to look and write it down.
Death begins life's whole routine to-do
in these stories of our fellow citizens.

Nobody saw it happen, or everyone saw,
but can't remember the car. What difference does it make
when the child will never fall in love, the girl will never
have a child, the man will never see a grandchild, the old maid
will never have another cup of hot cocoa at bedtime?
Like life, the dead are dead, their consciousness,
as dear to them as mine to me, snuffed out.
What has mind to do with this, when the earth is bereaved?

I lie, with my dear ones, holding a fictive umbrella,
while around us falls the real and acid rain.
The handle grows heavier and heavier in my hand.
Unlike life, tomorrow night under the bedlamp
by a quick link of thought someone will find out why,
and the policemen and their wives and I will feel better.
But all that's toward the end of the book. Meantime, tonight,
without a clue I enter sleep's little rehearsal.

My Father Gets Up in the Middle of the Night to Watch an Old Movie

Dennis Trudell

On cable television. Because he can't sleep.
My father gets up in the middle of the night
to watch an old movie on cable television—
because he can't sleep. He has done this before.
He will do it again, and sometimes he eats
cookies. My father eating cookies and watching
an old movie again because he can't sleep.
He is eighty-seven years old. He lives alone.
Because my mother died . . . and sometimes he looks
at her absence on the black sofa. My father
turning back to the movie on cable television,
eating another cookie. The movie has a name,
but he doesn't know it. My mother died—
because this is not a movie with a happy
ending. Or any ending. My father returns
to bed and goes to sleep. Or does not,
and then later sleeps. The television reflects
the lamp he leaves on . . . the black sofa.
Reflects an old mirror behind the sofa—

A Prayer in the Prospect of Death

Robert Burns

O Thou unknown Almighty Cause
  Of all my hope and fear!
In whose dread presence, ere an hour,
  Perhaps I must appear!

If I have wander'd in those paths
  Of life I ought to shun;
As something, loudly in my breast,
  Remonstrates I have done;

Thou know'st that Thou hast formed me
  With passions wild and strong;
And list'ning to their witching voice
  Has often led me wrong.

Where human weakness has come short,
  Or frailty stept aside,
Do thou, All-Good! For such Thou art,
  In shades of darkness hide.

Where with intention I have err'd,
  No other plea I have,
But Thou art good; and Goodness still
  Delighteth to forgive.

Diner

Louis Jenkins

The time has come to say goodbye, our plates empty except for our greasy napkins. Comrades, you on my left, balding, middle-aged guy with a ponytail, and you, Lefty, there on my right, though we barely spoke I feel our kinship. You were steadfast in passing the ketchup, the salt and pepper, no man could ask for better companions. Lunch is over, the cheese-burgers and fries, the Denver sandwich, the counter nearly empty. Now we must go our separate ways. Not a fond embrace, but perhaps a hearty handshake. No? Well then, farewell. It is unlikely I'll pass this way again. Unlikely we will all meet again on this earth, to sit together beneath the neon and fluorescent calmly sipping our coffee, like the sages sipping their tea underneath the willow, sitting quietly, saying nothing.

When Death Comes

Mary Oliver

When death comes
like the hungry bear in autumn;
when death comes and takes all the bright coins from his purse

to buy me, and snaps the purse shut;
when death comes
like the measle-pox;

when death comes
like an iceberg between the shoulder blades,

I want to step through the door full of curiosity, wondering:
what is it going to be like, that cottage of darkness?

And therefore I look upon everything
as a brotherhood and a sisterhood,
and I look upon time as no more than an idea,
and I consider eternity as another possibility,

and I think of each life as a flower, as common
as a field daisy, and as singular,

and each name a comfortable music in the mouth,
tending, as all music does, toward silence,

and each body a lion of courage, and something
precious to the earth.

When it's over, I want to say: all my life
I was a bride married to amazement.
I was the bridegroom, taking the world into my arms.

When it's over, I don't want to wonder
if I have made of my life something particular, and real.
I don't want to find myself sighing and frightened,
or full of argument.

I don't want to end up simply having visited this world.

At My Funeral

Willis Barnstone

I take a seat in the third row
and catch the eulogies. It's sweet
to see old friends, some I don't know.
I wear a tie, good shoes, and greet
a stranger with a kiss. It's bliss
for an insecure guy to hear
deep words. I'll live on them, not miss
a throb, and none of us will fear
the night. There are no tears, no sad
faces, no body or sick word
of God. I sing, have a warm chat
with friends gone sour, wipe away bad
blood. And sweet loves? I tell a bird
to tip them off. Then tip my hat.

The Wish to Be Generous

Wendell Berry

All that I serve will die, all my delights,
the flesh kindled from my flesh, garden and field,
the silent lilies standing in the woods,
the woods, the hill, the whole earth, all
will burn in man's evil, or dwindle
in its own age. Let the world bring on me
the sleep of darkness without stars, so I may know
my little light taken from me into the seed
of the beginning and the end, so I may bow
to mystery, and take my stand on the earth
like a tree in a field, passing without haste
or regret toward what will be, my life
a patient willing descent into the grass.

Last Poem

Ted Berrigan

Before I began life this time
I took a crash course in Counter-Intelligence
Once here I signed in, see name below, and added
Some words remembered from an earlier time,
"The intention of the organism is to survive."
My earliest, & happiest, memories pre-date WW II
They involve a glass slipper & a helpless blue rose
In a slender blue single-rose vase: Mine
Was a story without a plot. The days of my years
Folded into one another, an easy fit, in which
I made money & spent it, learned to dance & forgot, gave
Blood, regained my poise, & verbalized myself a place
In Society. 101 St. Mark's Place, apt. 12A, NYC 10009
New York. Friends appeared & disappeared, or wigged out,
Or stayed; inspiring strangers sadly died; everyone
I ever knew aged tremendously, except me. I remained
Somewhere between 2 and 9 years old. But frequent
Reification of my own experiences delivered to me
Several new vocabularies, I loved that almost most of all.
I once had the honor of meeting Beckett & I dug him.
The pills kept me going, until now. Love, & work,
Were my great happinesses, that other people die the source
Of my great, terrible, & inarticulate one grief. In my time
I grew tall & huge of frame, obviously possessed
Of a disconnected head, I had a perfect heart. The end

Came quickly & completely without pain, one quiet night as I
Was sitting, writing, next to you in bed, words chosen randomly
From a tired brain, it like them, suitable, & fitting.
Let none regret my end who called me friend.

10

SIMPLER THAN
I COULD FIND
WORDS FOR

Just Now

W. S. Merwin

In the morning as the storm begins to blow away
the clear sky appears for a moment and it seems to me
that there has been something simpler than I could ever
　　believe
simpler than I could have begun to find words for
not patient not even waiting no more hidden
than the air itself that became part of me for a while
with every breath and remained with me unnoticed
something that was here unnamed unknown in the days
and the nights not separate from them
not separate from them as they came and were gone
it must have been here neither early nor late then
by what name can I address it now holding out my thanks

Psalm 51

A psalm of David, when Nahum the prophet came unto him, after he had gone into Bathsheba.

Have mercy upon me, O God, according to your lovingkindness; according unto the multitude of your tender mercies blot out my transgressions. Wash me thoroughly from mine iniquity, and cleanse me from my sin. For I acknowledge my transgressions: and my sin is ever before me. Against you, you only, have I sinned, and done this evil in your sight: that you might be justified when you speak, and be clear when you judge. Behold, I was shapen in iniquity; and in sin did my mother conceive me. Behold, you desire truth in the inward parts: and in the hidden part you shall make me to know wisdom.

Purge me with hyssop, and I shall be clean: wash me, and I shall be whiter than snow. Make me to hear joy and gladness; that the bones which you have broken may rejoice. Hide your face from my sins, and blot out all mine iniquities. Create in me a clean heart, O God; and renew a right spirit within me.

Cast me not away from your presence; and take not your holy spirit from me. Restore unto me the joy of your salvation; and uphold me with your free spirit.

Then will I teach transgressors your ways; and sinners shall be converted unto you. Deliver me from bloodguiltness, O God of my salvation: and my tongue shall sing aloud of your righteousness.

O Lord, open my lips; and my mouth shall show forth your praise.

For you desire not sacrifice; else would I give it: you delight not in burnt offering. The sacrifices of God are a broken spirit: a broken and a contrite heart, O God, you will not despise.

Dawn Revisited

Rita Dove

Imagine you wake up
with a second chance: The blue jay
hawks his pretty wares
and the oak still stands, spreading
glorious shade. If you don't look back,

the future never happens.
How good to rise in sunlight,
in the prodigal smell of biscuits—
eggs and sausage on the grill.
The whole sky is yours

to write on, blown open
to a blank page. Come on,
shake a leg! You'll never know
who's down there, frying those eggs,
if you don't get up and see.

Crossing the Bar

Alfred, Lord Tennyson

Sunset and evening star,
    And one clear call for me.
And may there be no moaning of the bar,
    When I put out to sea,

But such a tide as moving seems asleep,
    Too full for sound and foam,
When that which drew from out the boundless deep
    Turns again home.

Twilight and evening bell,
    And after that the dark:
And may there be no sadness of farewell,
    When I embark;

For tho' from out our bourne of Time and Place
    The flood may bear me far,
I hope to see my Pilot face to face,
    When I have crost the bar.

Morning Swim

Maxine Kumin

Into my empty head there come
a cotton beach, a dock wherefrom

I set out, oily and nude
through mist, in chilly solitude.

There was no line, no roof or floor
to tell the water from the air.

Night fog thick as terry cloth
closed me in its fuzzy growth.

I hung my bathrobe on two pegs.
I took the lake between my legs.

Invaded and invader, I
went overhand on that flat sky.

Fish twitched beneath me, quick and tame.
In their green zone they sang my name

and in the rhythm of the swim
I hummed a two-four-time slow hymn.

I hummed "Abide With Me." The beat
rose in the fine thrash of my feet,

rose in the bubbles I put out
slantwise, trailing through my mouth.

My bones drank water; water fell
through all my doors. I was the well

that fed the lake that met my sea
in which I sang "Abide With Me."

Biographies

Virginia Hamilton ADAIR (1913–2004, Bronx, NY) grew up an only child in Montclair, New Jersey, and won prizes for the poetry she wrote as a student at Mount Holyoke. She married and had kids, and then was the first woman hired to teach at Cal Poly—she taught art history and English lit. She was 83 when her first book of poems, *Ants on the Melon*, was published. *I find rhyme is a handle on which to hang an incomplete memory.*

Fleur ADCOCK (1934, Papakura, New Zealand) grew up in England during WW II, which she wrote about later in *The Incident Book*, the experience of being an outsider, the "new girl." She attended university in New Zealand and, two marriages and two children later, moved back to England, where she worked as a librarian, then as a freelance writer and contributor to the BBC. Her *Poems 1960–2000* came out in 2000. *I certainly couldn't have stayed there. The mere thought of it frightens me to death. I would have gone mad. I have a slight phobia about being trapped in New Zealand without a return ticket.*

Kelli Russell AGODON (1971, Seattle, WA) was raised by a French Catholic mother and an atheist father in a Seattle suburb with a view of Mount Rainier. She left a 60-hour-a-week corporate job for the low-paying life of a poet and now writes from her home in Kitsap County, Washington. She published *Geography* in 2003 and *Small Knots* in 2004.

Allan AHLBERG (1938, South London) was a postman, grave digger, teacher and soldier before finding his niche as an author of children's books, including *The Bear Nobody Wanted*, *The Man Who Wore All His Clothes*, *It Was a Dark and Stormy Night*, and *The Jolly Postman, or Other People's Letters*. *My advice to young writers is to write. It's simple really.*

If you want to be a cyclist, you have to ride a bike. If you want the world record for eating pork pies, you have to eat pork pies. Just do it—whenever you feel like it—just for the fun of it.

Ginger ANDREWS (1956) was born in North Bend, Oregon, and lives there still, teaching Sunday school at the North Bend Church of Christ and cleaning houses for a living. Her first book, *An Honest Answer*, was published in 1999. *There's never a dull moment, though I'm praying for one.*

W. H. AUDEN (1907–1973) was born in York, England. His father was a physician, his mother a nurse and a High Anglican. ("Mother wouldn't like it," he often said, mockingly, in later life.) When he was eight, she taught him the great love duet in Wagner's *Tristan and Isolde*—he sang Isolde. By age 15 he knew he wanted to write, and at Oxford, he was a lackluster student and an ambitious poet. His visit to Berlin in the time of the Weimar Republic was a brief escape from repression (he wrote in his journal a list of "Boys had. Germany 1928–29"). Though homosexual, in 1935 he married Erika Mann so that she could get an English passport and escape from Germany, a generous act. He left England for America in 1939—for which he was accused of cowardice, though it was English society, the class system, his parents, the old order, more than the war, that he was escaping. His best-known poems—"September 1, 1939," "As I Walked Out One Evening," "In Memory of W. B. Yeats" and "To an Unknown Citizen"— all appeared in *Another Time* (1940)—except for his famous elegy, "Stop All the Clocks," from his play *The Ascent of F6* (1938). He lived in New York City, in St. Marks Place, a tireless teacher, essayist, editor, librettist (*The Rake's Progress*), playwright and poet, and a great wrinkly faced magistrate/patron of letters. In 1957, with the cash from an Italian literary prize, he bought a house and three acres in the village of Kirchstetten, Austria, where he spent part of each year and was very happy. He moved back to England the year before he died. *A poet is, before anything else, a person who is passionately in love with language.*

William BAER (1948, Wayne, NJ) holds three master's degrees— English from NYU, screen writing from USC and creative writing from Johns Hopkins—and a Ph.D. in English from the University of South Carolina. He teaches creative writing and cinema at Evansville University in Indiana, writes (his collection of poems, *"Borges" and Other Sonnets,* was published in 2003) and, with his wife Mona, edits *The Formalist,* a journal of metrical poetry he founded in 1990, when poets working in traditional forms—sonnet, villanelle, blank verse—had difficulty getting published. *The sonnet is like a faceted diamond, or a snowflake (always a hexagon), or a baseball diamond, or a chessboard set with its 32 pieces.*

Willis BARNSTONE (1927, Lewiston, ME) taught in Greece at the end of its civil war, in Buenos Aires during the Dirty War and in China during the Cultural Revolution. His 40 books include *The Secret Reader: 501 Sonnets;* a memoir biography, *With Borges on an Ordinary Evening in Buenos Aires;* and a translation of the New Testament, *The New Covenant: The Four Gospels and Apocalypse.* He teaches at Indiana University. *Writing has a psychological face. Let yourself go, be willing to go anywhere, and make dreams with eyes open.*

Jeanne Marie BEAUMONT (1954) grew up in suburban Philadelphia. At 29 she went off to New York to work in publishing and advertising, then to freelance. She teaches at Rutgers and at the 92nd Street Y. *The courage to build slowly / in the determined Roman way— / to knock off at sundown, / return the next day and the next.*

Hilaire BELLOC (1870–1953, La Celle-Saint-Cloud, France) was the son of a French lawyer and an English suffragist, known now mainly for his acerbic light verse, though a prolific writer of history, criticism, social commentary, travel essays, journalism of all sorts—someone called him "the man who wrote a library." His work fell into disfavor in large part because his conservative Catholic views were unfashionable. *When I am dead, I hope it is said, "His sins were scarlet, but his books were read."*

Ted BERRIGAN (1934–1983, Providence, RI) served in the U.S. Army in Korea, then attended the University of Tulsa before moving to New York City in the early sixties. He was of the New York School, which also included some friends of his from Tulsa—Ed Sanders, Ron Padgett and Jim Carroll. He died young after years of health problems from amphetamine use. His 20 books include *So Going Around Cities: New & Selected Poems 1958–1979* and a posthumous volume, *A Certain Slant of Sunlight*, poems designed to fit on a series of postcards. *Writing poetry is one of the things that human beings do, and can do. Writing poetry is how you tell your parents, your lover, all the people who don't know you and yourself, who you are, how you feel. . . . If you don't express yourself . . . you're a partly crippled individual.*

Wendell BERRY (1934, Port Royal, KY), the son of a tobacco farmer, got a couple of degrees in English at the University of Kentucky, taught at Stanford and NYU, went to Europe on a Guggenheim, before finally returning to Kentucky to write and farm full time on 250 acres along the Kentucky River near where it flows into the Ohio. His love for the land and sense of ecological responsibility shine in his poems and also in his crusading visionary essays collected in *The Long-Legged House* (1969), *The Gift of Good Land* (1981), *Home Economics* (1987), *What Are People For?* (1990), *Sex, Economy, Freedom, and Community* (1993) and *Another Turn of the Crank* (1995). *The past is our definition. We may strive, with good reason, to escape it, or to escape what is bad in it, but we will escape it only by adding something better to it.*

John BERRYMAN (1914–1972, McAlester, OK) graduated Phi Beta Kappa from Columbia in 1936, a protégé of Mark Van Doren, studied at Cambridge for two years, where he read Shakespeare and Yeats extensively, a high point in his life, and came home to begin his teaching career. His first collection, *Poems*, came out in 1942. He wrote important studies of Shakespeare, Thomas Nashe and Stephen Crane. His breakthrough book was *Homage to Mistress Bradstreet* in 1956, a dialogue between the poet and the ghost of Anne Bradstreet, his first of many books with Farrar, Straus and Giroux. And then there were *The Dream Songs*, 385 of them, starting in 1969. Despite a chaotic life, in and out of hospitals, darkened by the suicide of his father in 1926—a banker named John Smith who'd lost his shirt when the Florida land boom burst and then discovered his wife's affair with a man named Berryman (who might have murdered Smith) and who promptly married his wife—troubled by alcoholism, depression and romantic turmoil, he was an impassioned and steadfast teacher and writer to the end of his days, a suicide. *Being a poet is a funny kind of jazz. It doesn't get you anything. It doesn't get you any money, or not much, and it doesn't get you any prestige, or not much. It's just something you do.*

Elizabeth BISHOP (1911–1979, Worcester, MA) was a New Englander, orphaned young, a Vassar grad, independently wealthy, drawn to southern climes. Avoiding the confessional mode she wrote precisely and beautifully about the physical world in her small body of work—*The Complete Poems* (1969) numbers barely a hundred. She drew from her childhood in Nova Scotia—where she was raised by grandparents—her travels to Europe, her time in Key West and New York and 16 years in Brazil, living with Lota de Macedo Soares in Petrópolis, near Rio de Janeiro. Bishop was also an artist, and *Exchanging Hats* (1996) is a collection of more than 50 of her paintings. *All my life I have lived and behaved very much like the sandpiper—just running down the edges of different countries and continents, "looking for something."*

William BLAKE (1757–1827, London) was nine years old when he saw a tree full of angels, and in his adult life he often said that spirits would visit his studio to sit for portraits. He married Catherine Boucher, an illiterate woman, at the age of 25, and taught her to read, write and help him in his printing work. The two collaborated on his most famous works, his hand-illustrated poetry books *Songs of Innocence* and *Songs of Experience*. A friend once dropped by to find them sitting in their garden, naked, reciting passages from *Paradise Lost*. "Come in!" cried Blake. "It's only Adam and Eve, you know!" He died poor and unknown in London, coloring copies of his books while resting in bed. He was buried in an unmarked grave. *The man who never in his mind and thoughts travel'd to heaven is no artist.*

Robert BLY (1926, Madison, MN) was the son of Norwegian farmers ("I tried to become a playwright . . . the trouble was that nobody in my family talked") who, after the navy and Harvard, spent three years living down and out in New York, working odd jobs, sleeping in Grand

Central when necessary, writing incessantly. Determined to stay clear of universities, having discovered the work of Pablo Neruda, Cesar Vallejo, Georg Trakl and other major poets little known in literary academia, he moved back to Minnesota in 1955, to a farm near his parents', where he set out to promote foreign poets (and to insult the great sacred elephants of American Lit) in his magazine *The Fifties*, which became *The Sixties* and then *The Seventies*. His *Silence in the Snowy Fields* came out in 1962. A prolific writer and translator and tireless editor and performer and workshopper, he ventured far from poetic fields in his *Iron John: A Book About Men*, a treatise on the Grimm Brothers fairy tales, followed by *The Sibling Society* and (in collaboration with Marion Woodman) *The Maiden King*. His most recent works are *The Night Abraham Called to the Stars* and *My Sentence Was a Thousand Years of Joy*. *It is surely a great calamity for a human being to have no obsessions.*

Philip BOOTH (1925, Hanover, NH) lives on the coast of Maine, in Castine, in a house he lived in as a boy. His big collection is *Lifelines: Selected Poems, 1950–1999*.

Charles BUKOWSKI (1920–1994, Andernach, Germany) grew up poor in Los Angeles. He was a scrapper—abused by his father, scarred by acne and given to drink—who struggled to get published while earning a living as hospital orderly, elevator operator, poster hanger, truck driver, dishwasher, stockboy, shipping clerk and parking lot attendant. He wrote about hangovers, prostitutes, bums, his love of classical music and horse racing; his style is evident in the titles of his books: *Flower, Fist and Bestial Wail, Longshot Pomes for Broke Players, All the Assholes in the World and Mine, To Kiss the Worms Goodnight, Love Is a Dog from Hell, Septuagenarian Stew*. Black Sparrow Press was founded by his friend John Martin to publish Bukowski's work. *I don't like writers, but then I don't like insurance salesmen either.*

Robert BURNS (1759–1796, Alloway, Scotland) is the national poet of Scotland, born to a family of tenant farmers, a champion of the poor and downtrodden, an enemy of Scottish Calvinism. The people in his village thought he was odd because he read books as he drove his wagon slowly along the road. He loved traditional Scottish ballads, knew them by heart, and his *Poems, Chiefly in the Scottish Dialect*

(1786), which made his name, reflected that love. He had nine children, the last one born on the day of his funeral. *Or were I in the wildest waste, I Sae bleak and bare, sae bleak and bare, I The desert were a Paradise I If thou wert there, if thou wert there.*

Denver BUTSON (1965, Port Deposit, MD) lives and works in Brooklyn. He is a frequent collaborator with artists in other media, including photographer Cedric Chatterley and visual artist Pietro Costa on the book *grace*. His poems have been adapted for the stage and directed by Rhonda Keyser, and "The Effigy Café" was turned into a short film, directed by Kevin Doyle. . . . *the poems don't give me clarity when I write them. I get clarity when I hear someone respond to them.*

Thomas CAMPION (1567–1620, London) was orphaned early in life. He wrote and composed songs, took a short break in his forties to practice medicine, then returned to writing. King James commissioned him to write libretti for masques performed at court. He was questioned about the murder of Sir Thomas Overbury in 1615, but was found innocent and released. He never married and died in London, probably of the plague. *Poesy in all kind of speaking is the chiefe beginner, and maintayner of eloquence.*

Hayden CARRUTH (1921, Waterbury, CT) lived and wrote in Vermont and upstate New York (where he taught writing at Syracuse University). He is a prolific poet whose titles include *Collected Longer Poems*, *Collected Shorter Poems* and *Scrambled Eggs and Whiskey*. *You believe your writing can be a separate part of your life, but it can't. A writer's writing occurs in the midst of, and by means of, all the materials of life, not just a selected few.*

Raymond CARVER (1938–1988, Clatskanie, OR) grew up in Yakima, Washington, with hard-drinking, hardworking people, taking in difficult scenery that would later make its way into his writing. He married young, was working in a sawmill, when he took a few classes at Yakima Community College and got interested in poetry. He moved his young family to Paradise, California, and enrolled at Chico State, where he studied with the writer John Gardner. He joined the Iowa Writers' Workshop and quickly found success with his fiction, *Will You Please Be Quiet, Please?*, *Cathedral* and *What We Talk About When We Talk About Love*. But he had trouble with money and with his wife, and he drank. In 1977 he nearly died, quit drinking but made it through, met his future second wife, the poet Tess Gallagher, and turned his life around. He died, of lung cancer, at age 50. *Isak Dinesen said that she wrote a little every day, without hope and without despair. I like that.*

Susan CATALDO (1952–2001, Bronx, NY) was nine when she lost her mother to cancer, which became the subject of her second book, *The Mother Journal*. Her third book, *Drenched*, is a collection of poems. Both were published after she died of ovarian cancer about six months before her 49th birthday. *If my poetry is as important to you/ As our credit card payments then I You won't be hearing any love poems I From me for awhile.*

Richard CECIL (1944, Baltimore, MD) teaches at Indiana University. His latest collection, *Twenty First Century Blues*, came out in 2004. *"You've got talent but you lack ambition" I is not exactly what I'd call a fortune, I but as I hold it up to candlelight I I wag my head and chortle—That's me all right! I Whoever stuffed this message in my cookie I must have known it would be served to me I instead of to some self-promoting jerk I with zero skill, but lots of will to work.*

Elizabeth COATSWORTH (1893–1986) was born into a well-to-do family in Buffalo, New York. As a child and throughout her life she traveled, and far-away places show up in her poetry and her many children's books. She lived most of her life on a farm in Maine. *I have, quite deliberately, tried to make my writing clear, rather than rich, and as always happens when one chooses one path instead of another, I have lost by the choice as well as gained.*

Billy COLLINS (1941, New York, NY) served two terms as Poet Laureate of the United States (2001–2003). He teaches at Lehman College in the Bronx and runs Poetry 180, a program that encourages high school students to read a poem a day. As a high school student, he wrote a poem arguing that, since life is so miserable, babies should be killed off at birth. Later in life, he lightened up and wrote *The Apple That Astonished Paris* and *Sailing Alone Around the Room* and found great success as a performer of his own work. *One of the ridiculous aspects of being a poet is the huge gulf between how seriously we take ourselves and how generally we are ignored by everybody else.*

Wendy COPE (1945, Erith, Kent, England) studied history at St. Hilda's College in Oxford and became a best-selling author of light verse with *Bloody Men* and *Making Cocoa for Kingsley Amis*. Commissioned to write lines to be displayed in fireworks, she came up with "Write it in fire across the night: Some men are more or less alright." *I think it's a question which particularly arises over women writers: whether it's better to have a happy life or a good supply of tragic plots.*

Frances CORNFORD (1886–1960, Cambridge, England) was the granddaughter of Charles Darwin. Her son John was a poet and Communist who fought in the Spanish Civil War in the International Brigade and was killed near Madrid in 1936. *Magnificently unprepared for the long littleness of life.*

Noël COWARD (1899–1973, Teddington, Middlesex, England) was a popular playwright, songwriter and comic actor in both England and America with a "talent to amuse" who somehow did it for 50 years, from *Hay Fever* and *Private Lives* through his successful Las Vegas engagements and the revue *Cowardy Custard* toward the end of his life. He kept his homosexuality a well-known secret, refusing to come out, saying "A few old ladies in Brighton still don't know," though he wrote and acted in a play in 1966, *Song at Twilight*, in which an old gay writer worries about his sexuality being exposed. *Work hard, do the best you can, don't ever lose faith in yourself and take no notice of what other people say about you.*

Barbara CROOKER (1945, Cold Spring, NY) was a voracious reader as a child. She'd hide a book under her shirt when her parents forced her outdoors, crawl up the big willow tree in her front yard and continue reading. She lives in Fogelsville, Pennsylvania, with her husband and autistic son ("one of the most tenderhearted persons I know, and also one of the funniest"). She got started writing in her late twenties.

"I felt like I'd just stumbled through the underbrush onto a path that wasn't really clear, but there it was, and I've kept to it." Her most recent book is *Impressionism*. *I do feel poetry comes out of the deep places, where we are in touch with ourselves and our senses, and nature is, I think, the place where we are most alive, most tuned in.*

Edward Estlin CUMMINGS (1894–1962, Cambridge, MA) became e.e. cummings at Harvard. He enlisted as an ambulance driver in World War I, was detained by French authorities for six months, wrote a book about it (*The Enormous Room*) in 1922 and his first poems, whose romanticism was disguised by odd typography, began to appear soon after. He lived in Greenwich Village in New York and on a farm in North Conway, New Hampshire, where he died one fall, chopping wood. *Knowledge is a polite word for dead-but-not-buried imagination.*

Leo DANGEL (1941) was born and raised on a farm near Turkey Ridge, South Dakota. His collection *Old Man Brunner Country* was adapted for the stage.

Carl DENNIS (1939, St. Louis, MO) survived his early obsession with Yeats to write *A House of My Own* and *Practical Gods*. *[Poetry] is the medium or it's the kind of literature where you have the most intimate and direct relationship between writer and reader. You don't come at the reader with ideas and opinions, you try to bring a whole person into the poem.*

Emily DICKINSON (1830–1886, Amherst, MA) lived in her childhood home for her entire life, except for a year attending Mount Holyoke and brief trips to Boston, Philadelphia and Washington. Lively and sociable as a young woman, she became more and more reclusive, kept her writing a secret, experienced an intense and (it is supposed) imaginary love affair with the Reverend Charles Wadsworth and a long correspondence with Thomas Wentworth Higginson, who advised her not to publish. At her death, 1,775 poems were found in her papers, a few of which were published by her sister Lavinia in *Poems by Emily Dickinson*, in 1890. *Celebrity is the chastisement of merit and the punishment of talent.*

Gregory DJANIKIAN (1949, Alexandria, Egypt) is the son of Armenian parents who moved to the United States when he was eight. He lives in Williamsport, Pennsylvania, and is writing about the Armenian genocide of 1915, the first genocide of the 20th century. *It seems to me I can only make sense of my feelings toward the world when I sit down and try to articulate through language how I confront the world, how it confronts me, how I move through it.*

Stephen DOBYNS (1941, Orange, NJ) was a police reporter for the *Detroit News* and has written a popular series of mysteries, starring the detective Charlie Bradshaw. *I consider myself entirely a poet, am concerned with it twenty-four hours a day, feel that it requires that attention if one is to be successful, feel there is no subject which cannot be best treated by poetry, feel that myself and any poet is always at the beginning of his craft.*

John DONNE (1572–1631) was born in London to an affluent Catholic family, converted to Anglicanism as a young man and became an Anglican priest. His *Holy Sonnets* were written after his wife died while giving birth to their 12th child, a stillborn. *Art is the most passionate orgy within man's grasp.*

Catherine DOTY (1952, South Patterson, NJ) lives on Staten Island, New York. She is also a cartoonist and author of *Just Kidding, Cartoons for Grownups.*

Rita DOVE (1952, Akron, OH) is a former Poet Laureate of the United States, a singer, cellist and violist da gamba. She lives in Charlottesville, Virginia. *Music and poetry have much in common: the sense of a poem moves in and out of sync with the music of its language, which creates a marvelous kind of vibration—a frisson—and all unsaid things between those two poles keep a poem churning.*

Stephen DUNN (1939, New York, NY) was a professional basketball player, served in the U.S. Army, almost became a newspaperman, became a copywriter for Nabisco instead, then quit to write poetry. He teaches at Richard Stockton College of New Jersey. *It would be a lie to say I must choose between happiness and art. I can live with many things. Just to admit that I've been married for thirty-five years means that I've experienced joy and diminution and quiet evenings and tumultuous evenings and betrayal and dishonesty and tenderness and withholdings and forgiveness and cowardice and boredom and friendship.*

Gavin EWART (1916–1995, London) published his first poem, "Phallus in Wonderland," at age 17. His work was funny, and he was compared to Auden and Eliot, but then the war broke out and he put poetry on hold for 25 years, became an ad writer instead. When he started writing verse again, he quickly became the virtuoso comic poet of England, a bard of sex. His *The Pleasures of the Flesh* (1966) was banned from bookshops. *Success is a very small cake and poets are lucky to get a slice.*

James FENTON (1949, Lincoln, England) worked as a freelance reporter in Southeast Asia in the 1970s and covered the fall of Saigon and the rise of the Khmer Rouge in Cambodia. He translated Verdi's *Rigoletto*, transplanting it into the world of the New York mafia. His books include *Children in Exile: Poems 1968–1984*. *The writing of a poem is like a child throwing stones into a mine shaft. You compose first, then you listen for the reverberation.*

Lawrence FERLINGHETTI (1919, Yonkers, NY) became a pacifist when the navy sent him to Nagasaki six weeks after the atomic bomb was dropped. He studied art at the Sorbonne on the GI Bill and tried New York for a while, but ended up in San Francisco, which he said felt to him "a little like Dublin when Joyce was there." San Francisco was where he met the poet Kenneth Rexroth, an inspiration, and where he ventured into publishing and bookselling. He published Allen Ginsburg's *Howl*, which led to a famous obscenity trial, and his City Lights bookstore, at Broadway and Columbus in the North Beach section of San Francisco, is a famous tourist stop. His *A Coney Island of the Mind* (1958) was the best-selling book of poetry in the country during the sixties and seventies. *Like a bowl of roses, a poem should not have to be explained.*

Edward FIELD (1924, Brooklyn, NY) grew up on Long Island playing cello on the radio in the Field Family Trio. He fought in WW II, studied at NYU. He lives there still, writing poetry (*Magic Words: Poems* was published in 1997) and popular novels (his pseudonym is Bruce Elliot), editing anthologies, translating Eskimo stories and writing for film. *When I started writing, I wanted my poetry to save the world. It has to do with poetry as magic, the magic of words.*

Robert FRIEND (1913–1998, Brooklyn, NY) was born to Russian immigrants. He studied at Brooklyn College and spent most of his life traveling the world. He lived in Mexico, Guatemala, Switzerland, Spain, Italy, Colombia, Greece and Holland. He eventually settled in Israel in 1950, where he translated Hebrew poets into English. He also wrote poems about his beloved cats. His collections included *Salt Gifts* and *Somewhere Lower Down*. *The paradoxes of the intricately entwining meanings of "exile" and "home" may yet provide my major subject matter and produce, hopefully, real poems, so refuting Robert Lowell who once said that a poet must live in the country of his language.*

Robert FROST (1847–1963, San Francisco, CA) was a Dartmouth dropout, then a Harvard dropout. He considered drowning himself in the Great Dismal Swamp of Virginia, but married instead and took up farming in Derry, New Hampshire. His neighbors disapproved of his milking his cows in the middle of the night to avoid waking up early in the morning. But farming gave him something to write about. In 1915 he published *North of Boston*, which included many of his most famous poems: "Mending Wall," "The Death of the Hired Man," "Home Burial," "After Apple-Picking" and "The Wood-Pile." He went on to receive four Pulitzer Prizes (the most of any writer), and he was the first poet asked to read at an American presidential inauguration, John F. Kennedy's. *A poet never takes notes. You never take notes in a love affair.*

Erica FUNKHOUSER (1949, Concord, MA) teaches poetry at MIT. One of her poems, "Standing Up," was sandblasted into the wall of the Davis Square MBTA station in Somerville, Massachusetts. She also writes plays. *A really successful poem creates a new world first by obliterating the world in which we're sitting as we read the poem and then by substituting its own "green thought in a green shade."*

Leah FURNAS (1933, Trail, OR) grew up in her parents' tavern. She taught elementary school for 20 years, then sold real estate for the next 20, retired, took a poetry class and started writing. She wrote "The Longly-Weds Know" on a Steno pad bought at a gas station while driving to a friend's 50th wedding anniversary party. She lives in Coosbay, Oregon.

Elizabeth W. GARBER (1953, Belfast, ME) studied mythology and folklore at Harvard and Johns Hopkins. She is an acupuncturist in Belfast. Her first book, *Pierced by the Seasons: Living a Life on the Coast of Maine*, came out in 2004. *It's great to be surprised. That's what I love about poetry—it opens you up.*

George GARRETT (1929, Orlando, FL) is the author of a historical trilogy (*Death of the Fox, The Succession* and *Entered from the Sun*), cowriter of the movie *Frankenstein Meets the Space Monster* (1966) and a poet. He lives in Charlottesville with his wife. *One of the characteristics of the twentieth century is how often and how successfully we lie to ourselves.*

Sir W. S. GILBERT (1836–1911, London), the son of a surgeon, was a poet and playwright who joined with composer Arthur Sullivan to create *H.M.S. Pinafore* and *The Pirates of Penzance* and other light operas. *When everyone is somebody, then no one's anybody.*

Maria Mazziotti GILLAN (1940, Paterson, NJ) was born to Italian immigrants. Her *Italian Women in Black Dresses* deals with her working-class roots. *I want to write poems that make people laugh or cry or make the hair on their arms stand up. In order to write this kind of poem, you have to be willing to go to the deepest place inside yourself.*

William GREENWAY (1947, Atlanta, GA) is the son of a Southern Baptist preacher, a carpenter, a navy veteran, a teacher at Youngstown State in Ohio. *Perhaps because I was raised in the South, I care as much about how people say things as about what they say.*

R. S. GWYNN (1948, Eden, NC) played football at Davidson College and won awards for his writing. He lives in Beaumont, Texas. *There's nothing better than the feeling one gets when it's really humming along and it's 2 A.M. and that final line just falls into place.*

Donald HALL (1928, New Haven, CT) went to Phillips Exeter, Harvard, Oxford and Stanford, taught at the University of Michigan for 18 years, until 1975, when he moved with his wife, the poet Jane Kenyon, to the family farm in New Hampshire. He lives there still, though he lost Jane to cancer in 1995. His book of poems *Without* (1999) is about his coming to terms with her death. *I try every day to write great poetry as I tried when I was fourteen . . . What else is there to do?*

Barbara HAMBY (1952, New Orleans, LA) was born to a father who loved poetry and recited his favorite poems to her at bedtime. She teaches at Florida State. *Now Arabic, there's a poetic language, good-looking too, I like a river running through the fingers.*

Patricia HAMPL (1946, St. Paul, MN) is the daughter of a florist, was educated in a convent by nuns, studied piano performance before she became an English major. She lives in St. Paul, not far from where she grew up, scenes described in her memoir, *A Romantic Education*. *Memory is a great falsifier, and that's why it's a great fascinator. It's our most intimate and unbidden narrative power, partly because it connects things in a story form.*

Phebe HANSON (1928, Sacred Heart, MN) is the daughter of Norwegian immigrants, a poet and teacher. She taught for 40 years, starting in a one-room schoolhouse, and has kept a daily journal since 1941. Her first book, *Sacred Heart*, was published in 1985. *I'm sitting at my table, notebook open, Pilot Razor Point pen poised, / Gazing out my window at the snow-covered mountain ash in my courtyard, / Thinking of Munter, still painting in her eighties, even as I am still writing / This poem in my seventies, right now, for you.*

Thomas HARDY (1840–1928) was born in Dorset, England, and played fiddle for dances and weddings at age nine. When he was a teenager, he witnessed the public execution of a woman. He was an architect before taking up writing as a profession. *Poetry is emotion put into measure. The emotion must come by nature, but the measure can be acquired by art.*

Jim HARRISON (1937, Grayling, MI) is the son of a county ag agent. He has written 11 books of poetry and seven novels, including

Legends of the Fall, and various screenplays. He lives with his wife, Linda, in Montana and Arizona. *The only advice I can give to aspiring writers is don't do it unless you're willing to give your whole life to it. Red wine and garlic also help.*

Jennifer Michael HECHT (1965, Long Island, NY) is the author of *Doubt: A History* and *The End of the Soul: Scientific Modernity, Atheism, and Anthropology*. She lives in the East Village in New York City with her husband, John, and her son, Max. *I think I'm always writing in part to speak widely, to society or to history, and in part to speak privately: I'm just writing to myself, reminding myself of things.*

Adrian HENRI (1932–2000, Birkenhead, Cheshire, England) was a painter, poet and musician, one of the founding members of the band the Scaffold, and of the Grimms. *A poem has to be good enough to stand up in the cold light of day.*

Bob HICOK (1960, Lansing, MI) was an automotive die designer before he moved on to writing and teaching English at Virginia Tech in Blacksburg, Virginia. *I'm just not happy when I don't write. It's about my favorite thing to do. It's the unifying activity of my life. So when I don't write, I am, in the most basic sense, not being myself.*

Tony HOAGLAND (1953, Fort Bragg, NC) teaches at the University of Houston. His books include *What Narcissism Means to Me* (2003) and *Donkey Gospel* (1998). *A really good poem is the poem which breaks through the television screen into the world and reminds the reader that poetry is about open-heart surgery, being woken up, or taken somewhere unexpected and dangerous.*

Bill HOLM (1943, Minneota, MN) grew up on a farm among Icelanders. He put himself through college playing ragtime piano, lived in Iceland for a few years on a Fulbright and taught English in China. He travels extensively and spends his summers in Iceland. *There's a musical metaphor in almost all of my books.*

Meredith HOLMES (1949, Philadelphia, PA) lives in Cleveland Heights, Ohio, writing and editing freelance.

David IGNATOW (1914–1997) was born in Brooklyn, New York, and worked for many years in his father's bookbindery until 1965, when Wendell Berry offered him a job teaching at the University of Kentucky. He went on to teach at NYU, Columbia, the New School and Vassar, and to publish 16 volumes of poetry and three prose collections. *I'm lonely most of the time. I'm always after company. I guess when I'm writing I feel I've suddenly made company with myself. You become your own guest.*

Josephine JACOBSEN (1908–2003) was raised in the United States by her Canadian parents and lived most of her life in Maryland. She was poetry consultant to the Library of Congress, 1971–1973. *I am suspicious of all translations of poetry.*

Louis JENKINS (1942, Oklahoma City, OK) lives in Duluth, Minnesota. *I've been thinking of retiring, of selling the poetry business and enjoying my twilight years. . . . Maybe I'll do a little traveling, winter in the Southwest. Take up golf. Spend more time with the family. Maybe I'll just walk around and look at things with absolutely no compulsion to say anything at all about them.*

Ben JONSON (1572–1637, Westminister, London) was an actor and playwright who, in 1598, killed another actor in a duel, was tried for murder and escaped the gallows, though his thumb was branded with a felon's mark. *Who casts to write a living line, must sweat.*

John KEATS (1795–1821, Finsbury Pavement, England) was the son of a livery-stable keeper. He quit his medical education to pursue a literary career. When his health failed, his doctor ordered him to Italy, where he died of tuberculosis in 1821. *There is nothing stable in the world; uproar's your only music.*

X. J. KENNEDY (1929, Dover, NJ) was born shortly before the stock market crash. Christened Joseph, he added the X to his name for variety's sake. He spent four years in the navy as an enlisted journalist, serving aboard destroyers. He has written verse and fiction for children, and he and his wife, Dorothy, edited *Knock at a Star: A Child's Introduction to Poetry*. His first book was *Nude Descending a Staircase* in 1961. He lives in Lexington, Massachusetts. *I don't ever think about my self-identity as a poet. Honest.*

Jane KENYON (1947–1995) spent half her life in Ann Arbor and half in Eagle Pond, New Hampshire, with her husband, Donald Hall. *There are things in life that we must endure which are all but unendurable, and yet I feel that there is a great goodness. Why, when there could have been nothing, is there something? This is a great mystery. How, when there could have been nothing, does it happen that there is love, kindness, beauty?*

Stuart KESTENBAUM (1951, New Jersey) is the director of Haystack Mountain School of Crafts in Deer Isle, Maine, where he coteaches classes combining pottery and poetry. He is the author of two collections of poetry, *Pilgrimage* and *House of Thanksgiving. Watching people work with clay and metal and wood has given me a way to see words as materials in a similar way.*

Galway KINNELL (1927, Providence, RI) grew up in Pawtucket. He went to Princeton, where he roomed with W. S. Merwin, then served in the navy, went to Paris on a Fulbright, worked in voter registration in the South, traveled widely in the Middle East and Europe, taught here and there. His first book was *What a Kingdom It Was* (1960), followed by *Flower Herding on Mount Monadnock, Body Rags, The Avenue Bearing the Initial of Christ into the New World: Poems 1946–1965* and others. *It is the dream of every poem to be a myth.*

Ted KOOSER (1939, Ames, IA) was vice president of Lincoln Benefit Life, an insurance company, and wrote in the morning before heading to work. He lives in Lincoln, Nebraska, with his wife, Kathleen. In 2004 he was chosen as the U.S. Poet Laureate, the first from the Great Plains. *I was informed by a phone call. I was so staggered I could barely respond. The next day, I backed the car out of the garage and tore the rearview mirror off the driver's side.*

Steve KOWIT (1938, Brooklyn, NY) lives in the San Diego backcountry near the Mexican border and teaches at Southwesteren College in Chula Vista. *I love poetry of compassion, poetry about the state of the world, not just the state of the poet's family, friends, personal memories and genital concerns. A poetry of compassion means feeling deeply for other beings. We are, when all is said and done, a savage, unappetizing little species whose most salient collective char-*

acteristic is a murderous hatred of the out-group. . . . So it's terribly useful when we find poets who can remind us to feel deeply for the rest of the world.

Maxine KUMIN (1925, Philadelphia, PA) is the daughter of a pawn-broker who went to Radcliffe, met her husband, Victor, and married him in 1946 and 11 years later enrolled in a poetry workshop in Boston, where she met and became friends with Anne Sexton. Maxine Kumin is a prolific writer of novels, short stories, more than 20 children's books, four books of essays, memoirs (*Inside the Halo* and *Beyond: The Anatomy of Recovery*) and 11 books of poetry (her first collection, *Halfway*, came out in 1961). And crime fiction. She lives on a horse farm in New Hampshire. *There is no more, no less, peace of mind in the disciplined life of the barnyard than there is in the routine of the office.*

Naomi LAZARD (East Hampton, NY) is a playwright and cofounder of the Hamptons International Film Festival. She started writing poetry at 25, in a workshop at the University of Chicago after studying graphic design at the Institute of Design. She's published books of her own poems (like *Cry of the Peacocks*) and of her translations (like *The True Subject*, a translation of Faiz Ahmed Faiz from the Urdu). *Writing a play is the same process as writing a poem, everything happens in the present, the writing goes from peak to peak, all show no tell. Oh, and the voice is everything.*

Jack LaZebnik (1913–2004) grew up in Jackson, Michigan, where his father was in the scrap business. He flew B-24 Liberators in the air force in WW II, went to the University of Michigan and then studied, with his wife, Vesta, at the Sorbonne. He taught at Stephens College in Columbia, Missouri. *Without suffering, there's no conflict; without conflict, no drama; without drama, no meaning.*

Kate LIGHT (1960, Illinois) is a violinist in the New York City Opera orchestra and the author of a concert piece about the deep sea, *Oceanophony*, which she narrates. *I am drawn to—but not exclusive about—form, enjoying the dialogue between the traditional and the contemporary. I do wish, above all, to be specific, conversational, and clear. Punctuation, spacing, and italics are cherished tools of phrasing, timing, and dynamics, as in music, or, for that matter, in speech.*

Gerald LOCKLIN (1941, Rochester, NY) teaches at California State at Long Beach. He was the brave man who first brought Charles Bukowski to a university to read and was an early proponent of "stand-up poetry"—poetry as entertainment, jokey, vernacular, autobiographical. *Bukowski wasn't really someone you would want to be around when he had been drinking a lot.*

Diane LOCKWARD (Montclair, NJ) was a high school English teacher for 20 years and now works as a poet-in-the-schools for the New Jersey Writer's Project and the Geraldine R. Dodge Foundation. She published *Eve's Red Dress*, her first full-length book, in 2003. She lives in West Caldwell, New Jersey, with her husband and writes in the morning so she can revise all day and night. *I like the quality of strangeness in poetry and try to get there via free association and daydreaming.*

Henry Wadsworth LONGFELLOW (1807–1882, Portland, ME) graduated from Bowdoin College at age 19, a classmate of Nathaniel Hawthorne's, and spent the next three years touring Italy, Spain, England, France and Germany, polishing his command of languages. In grief after the death of his first wife in 1835, he settled for a time in Heidelberg. He taught at Harvard and the "spreading chestnut tree" of his poem "A Village Blacksmith" was on Brattle Street in Cambridge. *Look, then, into thine heart and write.*

Kilian McDONNELL (1921, Great Falls, MT) grew up in Velva, North Dakota. He has been a Benedictine monk and priest for more than 50 years and founded the Institute for Ecumenical and Cultural Research at St. John's University. He started writing poetry at the age of 75. *I do not write pious or inspirational verse. I write about confronting God. Like Jacob, I wrestle with Yahweh, but, unlike Jacob, I never prevail and I walk away limping.*

Jo McDOUGALL (1935) grew up on a rice farm in the Arkansas Delta near DeWitt and lives in Little Rock. Her son, Duke, suffered a stroke in 1996, and in 1999 her daughter, Charla, died of cancer.

Southerners are more talkative and dramatic and tend to celebrate the strange. I like the strange but I'm also attracted to the stoicism of midwestern attitudes. I became more grounded in the landscape. I think living in the Midwest has influenced me to write tighter poems.

Heather McHUGH (1948, San Diego, CA) was born to Canadian parents and maintains dual citizenship. She and her husband, Nicolai Popov, have translated poems from Bulgarian, his native language. She lives in Seattle and has a Web site (www.spondee.com) where her e-poems appear. *You need the scroll function for that poem to work. Isn't it a kick that scrolls and icons are back??? I love the lingo.*

Wesley McNAIR (1941, Newport, NH) grew up in public housing outside of Springfield, Vermont, where his mother took in sewing and cut hair to support him and his two brothers. He worked on farms, married young, taught school, was "perpetually broke and in debt" but preserved his mornings for writing poetry. *I would like my poems to be read by ordinary people.*

Louis MacNEICE (1907–1963), a Belfast boy, son of an Anglican rector, wrote about his boyhood in his famous poem "Carrickfergus." He went to Oxford ("a delectable reprieve"), was a friend of Auden's, a teacher of Greek and philosophy and for 20 years a staff writer for the BBC. He wrote radio plays and poetry and translated Goethe and Aeschylus. *There is material for poetry everywhere; the poet's business is not to find it but to limit it.*

Don MARQUIS (1878–1937, Walnut, IL) was a columnist for the New York *Sun*, where he introduced the cockroach Archie, a reincarnation of a poet laureate, and the free-spirited cat Mehitabel. *Publishing a volume of verse is like dropping a rose petal down the Grand Canyon and waiting for the echo.*

Andrew MARVELL (1621–1678, Yorkshire, England) was a close friend of Milton's, who helped him get the job of Assistant Latin Secretary to the Council of State, which led to Marvell's career in Parliament and the diplomatic corps: he served in Holland and Russia. His "To His Coy Mistress" was written around 1650 and published only after his death. *Let us roll all our strength, and all / Our sweetness, up into one ball: / And tear our pleasures with rough strife, / Through the iron gates of life.*

Herman MELVILLE (1819–1891) was born in New York City to an established merchant family. His father went bankrupt and insane and died when Herman was 12. When Herman was 20, he shipped out as a cabin boy on the whaler *Acushnet*. He wrote his 1851 masterpiece *Moby-Dick* in about a year at his farm near Pittsfield, Massachusetts, and dedicated it to his friend Nathaniel Hawthorne. It did not sell as well as his earlier adventure books *Typee* and *Omoo*. *We cannot live for ourselves alone. Our lives are connected by a thousand invisible threads, and along these sympathetic fibers, our actions run as causes and return to us as results.*

W. S. MERWIN (1927, New York, NY) is the son of a Presbyterian minister ("I started writing hymns for my father as soon as I could write at all") and grew up in Union City, New Jersey, and Scranton, Pennsylvania, then was scholarshipped into Princeton. He studied Romance languages there, which helped him make his way in the world as a translator (French, Spanish, Portuguese, Latin) and as a poet. He is the author of more than 15 books of poetry and nearly 20 books of translation, including Dante's *Purgatorio*, as well as plays and prose, including his memoir of life in the south of France, *The Lost Upland*. He resides in a jungly paradise in Hawaii, on a hillside on which he has planted hundreds of palm trees. *I went to see Ezra Pound when I was nineteen or so. He told me something that I think I really already knew. He said that it was important to regard writing as not a chance or romantic or inspired (in the occasional sense) thing, but rather a kind of spontaneity which arises out of discipline and continual devotion to something.*

Edna St. Vincent MILLAY (1892–1950, Rockland, ME) was the shining red-haired heroine of bohemian fame in the twenties, famous for her insouciance, her romances with men and women, her bravado ("Soar, eat ether, see what has never been seen; depart, be lost, but climb"), her feminism. In 1923, she married Eugen Boissevain, who managed her literary career and set up the readings and public appearances for which she grew quite famous. *I am glad that I paid so little attention to good advice; had I abided by it I might have been saved from some of my most valuable mistakes.*

Robert MORGAN (1944, Hendersonville, NC) grew up on the family farm in the Green River Valley of the Blue Ridge Mountains. He studied engineering at N.C. State, then switched to UNC–Chapel Hill, where he majored in English. He wrote only poetry for years and then two novels set in western Carolina, *Gap Creek* and *The Truest Pleasure*, which have attracted millions of readers. *We tend to write best about cultures that have almost melted into the past. The blue valleys, the fog-haunted coves, the tireless milky waterfalls, are still there, but the people, the people with wisdom in their hands and humility in their hearts, have slipped away forever, unless we find them in our own words, and in our own hands and hearts. . . . I tried to communicate the mystery and fear, the terror and resentment, the harshness and futility, the contradictions and cruelties, as well as the loyalties and kinships and beauties, of the world I had grown up in. . . . I was never interested in portraying a pastoral world, a simpler world, but in dramatizing the complexities of the seemingly plain, the sharpness of the everyday, the cruelties of the conventional, the isolation of the rural. I wanted to show the thresholds of the theatrical in the ordinary.*

Lisel MUELLER (1924, Hamburg, Germany) moved with her family to the Midwest when she was 15 after her father was forced to flee the Nazis. As a sociology major at the University of Evansville, she was inspired by Carl Sandburg, "because English was still relatively new to me, and Sandburg, of course, wrote in a very easy-to-understand, very colloquial and informal manner." In 1997, she won a Pulitzer for *Alive Together*. She lives in Lake Forest, Illinois, 35 miles outside Chicago, in a house that she built with her husband 40 years ago. *Make up your own / ending, you say to the children, / and they will, they will.*

Leonard NATHAN (1924, Los Angeles, CA) has written nine books of poetry (*Western Reaches, Holding Patterns*) and has translated the work of many poets. He lives in Kensington, California, and has taught rhetoric at Berkeley since 1960. *The older I get, the more I find myself revisiting childhood in my poetry and discovering myself at home again in a world like that of folk or fairy tales, where the strange can become familiar, the familiar strange.*

Howard NEMEROV (1920–1991, New York, NY) grew up in New York, graduated from Harvard in 1941 and went from there to the air force, where he was a bomber pilot. After the war he began teaching, first at Hamilton, then Bennington, then at Washington University in St. Louis, where he stayed for 32 years. He wrote novels, plays and criticism, as well as poetry. *Language is remarkable in that, except under the extreme constraints of mathematics and logic, it never can talk only about what it's supposed to talk about but is always spreading around so that the lovers, the commonwealth, the economy, they all get mixed into the act in a very—this term must come from cooking—in a very "meddled" way.*

William NOTTER (1971, Cobleskill, NY) grew up on a dairy farm in eastern Colorado, moved to Mississippi after college, made a living picking cotton, pouring concrete, fixing tires, digging post holes, got his MFA in poetry from the University of Arkansas. He teaches in Reno and drag races. *I have always been drawn to open places (maybe more so after living in the South) like the high plains, the Utah canyon country and Wyoming's alpine meadows.*

Alden NOWLAN (1933–1983) was born to a 14-year-old mother and a gadabout alcoholic father, a one-dollar-a-day laborer, in Nova Scotia. He attended school only up to the fifth grade but educated himself, became a journalist at the *Observer* and the *Telegraph Journal* in St John, New Brunswick, and then writer in residence at the University of New Brunswick. *Many, many times since I was a very small child I've stopped for a moment and thought to myself how very strange it is to be alive, that recurrent feeling of naked wonder.*

Sharon OLDS (1942, San Francisco, CA) was raised as a "hellfire Calvinist," went to Stanford, then leaped the country to earn her Ph.D. at Columbia, vowed to become a poet and settled on the Upper West Side of New York. Her first book was *Satan Says* in 1980. *I'm trying to get out of art's way. Not trying to look good, if a poem's about me. Not trying to look bad. Not asking a poem to carry a lot of rocks in its pockets. But just being an ordinary observer and liver and feeler and letting the experience get through you onto the notebook with the pen, through the arm, out of the body, onto the page, without distortion.*

Mary OLIVER (1935, Maple Heights, OH) lives in Vermont and Cape Cod. She worked at her writing for 25 years before publishing a book, rising at 5 A.M., avoiding writing workshops and such, avoiding interesting jobs lest she be distracted from her mission. *If anybody has a job and starts at 9, there's no reason why they can't get up at 4:30 or 5 and write for a couple of hours, and give their employers their second-best effort of the day—which is what I did.*

Ron PADGETT (1942, Tulsa, OK) was the son of bootleggers. He started writing poetry at age 13 and in high school started *The White Dove Review*, which published Ginsberg, Kerouac, Creeley and others. In 1960, he moved to New York to attend Columbia. He spent a year studying in Paris, then moved back to New York, to the East Village, where he still lives. He has spent many years teaching poetry writing to children and also writing on the subject. *The greatest invention of all time is the remote control. The quick cutting we used to see only in avant-garde films is now commonplace. Those fast images help form the thinking patterns of the people who grow up looking at them. . . . Unfortunately it seems to bring with it a loss in our ability to think in large structures—big paragraphs with complicated sentences.*

Grace PALEY (1922, New York, NY) is a bard of Jewish New York and the author of phenomenal books like *The Little Disturbances of Man* and *Enormous Changes at the Last Minute*. She taught at Sarah Lawrence for years. She describes herself as a "somewhat combative pacifist and cooperative anarchist." *The word "career" is a divisive word. It's a word that divides the normal life from business or professional life.*

Linda PASTAN (1932, New York, NY) grew up in the Bronx, near the intersection of Fordham Road and the Grand Concourse, near Alexander's Department Store and Poe's cottage, the granddaughter of Jewish immigrants from eastern Europe. She went to Radcliffe and Brandeis.

The Last Uncle is her most recent book, preceded by *Carnival Evening, An Early Afterlife* and *Heroes in Disguise*. She lives in Potomac, Maryland. *When the world of money, fame, and literary politics manages to get to me, I remember what Tennessee Williams wrote: "The only honor you can confer upon a writer is a good morning's work."*

Stanley PLUMLY (1939, Barnesville, OH) grew up in Ohio and Virginia and studied at Ohio University. He started writing poems when he was 19, trying to come to terms with an alcoholic father who died young. ("I can hardly think of a poem I've written that at some point in its history did not implicate, or figure, my father.") He teaches English at the University of Maryland. *There is a lot of writing that is very self-referential. I believe, however, in something Randall Jarrell called dailiness—the sense of the detail or object in front of you that wants to be transformed. But I also believe strongly in the archetype, the larger figure outlining the smaller figure. I believe in poetry's philosophical discourse, the verity of the universal or common. In that sense I guess I'm a romantic.*

Lawrence RAAB (1946, Pittsfield, MA) is a poet, screenwriter and playwright, translator, critic, and essayist, professor of English at Williams College and author of *What We Don't Know About Each Other*. *No matter what I have invested in each poem personally, I want to put voices on the page that can go out in the world without explanations.*

Christopher REID (1949, Hong Kong) is the son of an oil company executive. Educated in England, he was poetry editor of Faber & Faber before going freelance. *Ignorance is one of youth's great assets, isn't it? You do things, thinking they're new, little realizing that they've been done a hundred times before, in slightly different forms that you weren't able to recognize. . . . What I have never understood is the sense of shame that attaches to rhyme, in certain minds. It's a Puritan thing, isn't it? In this debate, I'm decidedly a Cavalier.*

Kenneth REXROTH (1905–1982, South Bend, IN) was born to an Indiana family of socialists and freethinkers. He was self-educated, a painter, a theater man, orphaned at 14; he lived with relatives in Chicago, hitchhiked around the country, traveled to Europe, emigrated to San Francisco in 1927. He chose San Francisco, he said, because it was not settled by Puritans but by gamblers, prostitutes, rascals and fortune seekers, and also because it was near the mountains, where he loved to spend months at a time, backpacking, rock climbing, skiing, fly-fishing. He pursued eastern mysticism, leftist politics, ecological awareness and erotic art. He rallied to the cause of Japanese Americans held in internment camps, protested all wars, promoted Ferlinghetti and other poets on his KPFA radio show and was a patron of the Beat poets of the fifties, though he scorned the notion of Beatdom as a creation of *Time* and *Life*. He championed poetry through his magazine columns and anthologies. *Man thrives where angels would die of ecstasy and where pigs would die of disgust.*

Lee ROBINSON (1948, Charlotte, NC) earned a B.A. in philosophy, then a law degree from Antioch. She was a legal aid lawyer, public defender, then practiced privately in Charleston, South Carolina. She moved to Texas in 1998 and lives on a ranch in the hill country with her husband. *There's no such thing as the necessary poem; that's what saves poetry from a life like ours, from desire and striving. . . . The poem is redeemed by indifference, that before it's written, the world does very well without it. Therefore it is free to be what it wants to be or not to be at all.*

Carl SANDBURG (1878–1967, Galesburg, IL) was born to Swedish immigrants, Clara and August. The second of seven children, he quit school after the eighth grade and worked odd jobs delivering milk, harvesting ice, laying bricks, threshing wheat and shining shoes before traveling the country for a year as a hobo at age 19, which sharpened his leftist views. He met his wife while working for the Wisconsin Social Democratic Party. He was writing editorials for the Chicago *Daily News* when Harriet Monroe, the founder of *Poetry* magazine, discovered his verse and encouraged him to persist, which led to his first book, *Chicago* (1916), then *Cornhuskers* (1918) and *Smoke and Steel* (1920). A journalist, poet, folksinger, biographer of Abraham Lincoln (in six volumes), his work slipped into disrepute after his death, a reaction against his great celebrity for much of his life. *Here is the difference between Dante, Milton, and me. They wrote about hell and never saw the place. I wrote about Chicago after looking the town over for years and years.*

Robyn SARAH (1949, New York, NY) was born to Canadian parents and grew up in Montreal, where she lives today. She studied clarinet at the Conservatoire de Musique et d'Art Dramatique du Québec and philosophy at McGill and cofounded a small press, Villeneuve Publications, in 1976. She writes widely for Canadian newspapers, book reviews, op-ed columns and taught college English for 20 years. *I started at such an early age, I almost can't remember a time when writing wasn't part of my identity. I was six, in first grade, just beginning to read, when my mother put an unexpected gift into my hands, a "Huge 10-cent Scribbler"—bright orange covers, ruled newsprint inside. "Here," she said, "it's a book for writing in. You can write a story in it."*

William SHAKESPEARE (1562–1616, Stratford-upon-Avon, England) was 23 when he went to London to act on the stage with the Queen's Company, then the Lord Chamberlain's Men, and then to author 17 comedies, 10 historical plays and 10 tragedies, prospering at this trade so that, by 1599, he owned a 10 percent share in the Globe Theater. In 1609, the *Sonnets* came out. In 1613, the Globe burned to the ground, set afire by a cannon fired during *Henry VIII* and the audience, absorbed in the play, did not notice until the curtains caught fire, then escaped without casualties. The theater was rebuilt by the following year. Shakespeare lived through two plagues, the defeat of the Spanish Armada, the death of Elizabeth I, the discovery of the Gunpowder Plot and the first English settlements of North America. *In winter's tedious nights sit by the fire with good old folks, and let them tell thee tales of woeful ages, long ago betid.*

David SHUMATE (1950, Iowa City, IA) lives in Zionsville, Indiana. *High Water Mark* was his first book of poems. *[Prose poetry] allows me to use narrative and lyrical elements in ways that line break poetry does not. I find that it corresponds to my breathing, to the cadence of my heart.*

Charles SIMIC (1938, Belgrade) came to the United States with his parents in 1953, grew up in Chicago, served in the army, then moved to New York, went to NYU, hung out with writers, did all sorts of jobs, wrote poems, collected them in books, won a slew of awards and fellowships, put together a career. He is the author of more than 60 books, including a memoir, *A Fly in the Soup*. He lives in New Hampshire. *One needs inspiration to write when one is twenty. At the age of sixty, there's the mess of one's entire life and little time remaining to worry about.*

Maurya SIMON (1950, New York, NY) began as an entomologist, studying the taxonomies of bugs, but found she preferred writing poems about bugs instead. She also writes about the black bears with whom she shares her mountain neighborhood in southern California. *All language is a masquerade. / But how we crave its bright feathers.*

Louis SIMPSON (1923, Kingston, Jamaica) was born to a Scottish father and Russian mother. He studied at Columbia, then went to war, serving in the 101st Airborne in France, Holland, Belgium and Germany. He was living in France when his first book, *Arrivistes*, came out in 1949. He got a Ph.D. at Columbia and went on to teach in California and New York and to write 17 books of poems and as many of prose, including fiction, criticism and a memoir, *The King My Father's Wreck*. *The aim of military training is not just to prepare men for battle, but to make them long for it.*

Hal SIROWITZ (1949, New York, NY) is a popular performance artist, the poet laureate of the borough of Queens and the author of *Mother Said* and *My Therapist Said* and *Father Said*. He worked for 25 years as a special education teacher for the New York City public schools. *Stuttering kind of changed my life. It made me an outsider, it made me a writer. It was harder to approach people, I had no control over it. It made me a witness of my own life. Instead of getting involved in life I would step back and watch it. So, I became an observer, which is good in a way, because you keep a record of your life. I have a record of who I am, I have a history.*

Gary SNYDER (1930, San Francisco, CA) is the bridge between the Beats and the backpackers. His first book, *Riprao* (1959), grew out of his experiences as a laborer at Yosemite and a lookout ranger. Sixteen books have followed, including *Mountains and Rivers Without End* and *Axe Handles*. Snyder says that one should live in one place, as an environmentally friendly deed, and know the native plants and animals and where your water comes from. He teaches at UC, Davis. *My sense of optimism has had the shit kicked out of it. But it's still kicking.*

Muriel SPARK (1918, Edinburgh, Scotland) was crowned Gillespie's High School for Girls' Queen of Poetry at age 14. Journalist and editor, then novelist, her *The Prime of Miss Jean Brodie* secured her literary reputation in 1962. She lives in Tuscany. *I had a love of writing which was becoming an imperative in my life. With an idea developing in my head, a pen in my hand and a notebook open before me I was in bliss.*

Debra SPENCER (1951, Culver City, CA) invented her own alphabet when she was three and attributes much of her writing to her father, who requested she write him a story at age six. She works at Cabrillo College as a learning disabilities specialist. She lives in the San Francisco Bay area with her sons and husband. *In 1990 I started walking every day (because of a bad back) and noticed that I got the best ideas for poems while walking and then forgot them. One day in desperation to remember, I scratched an idea on the inside of my forearm with my fingernail. It worked, but ever since then I've made sure I have some paper and a pen in my pocket.*

William STAFFORD (1914–1993, Hutchinson, KS) migrated from Kansas to Iowa to Oregon, where he taught for 32 years at Lewis and Clark College. His first major collection, published when he was 48, was *Traveling Through the Dark*, which won the National Book Award in 1963. *A writer is not so much someone who has something to say as he is someone who has found a process that will bring about new things he would not have thought of if he had not started to say them. That is, he does not draw on a reservoir; instead, he engages in an activity that brings to him a whole succession of unforeseen stories, poems, essays, plays, laws, philosophies, religions. . . .*

Clemens STARCK (1937, Rochester, NY)—carpenter by day, poet by night—wasn't published until he was 57. He majored in French lit at Princeton, dropped out after two years, found work as a newspaper reporter, then shipped off to the West Coast as a merchant seaman. He started writing poems in the mid-1970s, when he settled in Oregon, where he still lives with his wife. *Here I was making little models, little word models. And that proved absolutely fascinating.*

Gertrude STEIN (1874–1946, Allegheny, PA) grew up in Oakland— of which she famously said, *"There is no there there"*—and moved to Paris with her brother Leo in 1903. She lived with her lover, Alice B. Toklas, a relationship that lasted 39 years. Their home was a salon for artists (Picasso, Matisse, Braque) and writers (Anderson, Hemingway) between the wars. Her theory of writing, which is sometimes compared to Cubism in its repetition and fragmentation, is explained in her *Composition and Explanation.* Her best-known book was *The Autobiography of Alice B. Toklas* (1933), actually Stein's own autobiography, and her operas (music by Virgil Thomson) *Four Saints in Three Acts* and *The Mother of Us All* are still performed. *A writer should write with his eyes and a painter paint with his ears. I have always noticed that in portraits of really great writers the mouth is always firmly closed.*

Wallace STEVENS (1879–1955, Reading, PA) was a Harvard man, a lawyer and vice president for 20 years of the Hartford Accident and Indemnity Co. He wrote poems on his way to and from the office, based on ideas he usually came up with on his long walks. *The Collected Poems of Wallace Stevens* was published in 1954 to mark his 75th birthday, and he died the following year, the same year he won a Pulitzer. *It gives a man character as a poet to have this daily contact with a job.*

Robert Louis STEVENSON (1850–1894, Edinburgh, Scotland) was close to following in his father's footsteps and becoming an engineer, but decided at 21 that he'd rather be a writer. He wrote essays and travel articles, but didn't publish his first fiction, a short story, until he was 27. He wrote *Treasure Island* (1882), *Kidnapped* (1886) and *The Strange Case of Dr. Jekyll and Mr. Hyde* (1886), which made him famous around continental Europe and America. He hated Calvinist Scotland and preferred living a bohemian lifestyle abroad. He met his wife, Fanny Osbourne, an older American divorcée, in France and they traveled together through the American West and into the Pacific, finally settling in Samoa, where Robert lived and worked until tuberculosis took his life. *The difficulty of literature is not to write, but to write what you mean; not to affect your reader, but to affect him precisely as you wish.*

Susanna STYVE (1974, Minneapolis, MN) is an avid tennis player and lives in St. Paul. *I'll commiserate with any and all struggling writers because I know how tricky, sneaky and utterly manipulative the English language can be. . . . Make writing sport instead of torture.*

May SWENSON (1913–1989, Logan, UT), the oldest of 10 children of Mormon parents, moved to New York City as a young woman and spent her life editing, teaching poetry and writing poems about all kinds of things, including turtles, the subway and Long Island. *I wanted to make my poems do what they say.*

Alfred, Lord TENNYSON (1809–1892, Somersby, Lincolnshire, England) was the son of a clergyman who suffered from depression and alcoholism, and as a result Alfred worried about mental illness throughout his life. For his poetry, he was made a baron and is buried in Poets' Corner in Westminster Abbey. *Words, like nature, half reveal and half conceal the soul within.*

Dennis TRUDELL (1938, Buffalo, NY) lives in Madison, Wisconsin, with his wife. *Sloppy, raggedy-assed old life. I love it. I never want to die.*

Mona VAN DUYN (1921–2004) grew up in Waterloo, Iowa, and started writing poetry at the age of five. In 1992, she was named Poet Laureate of the United States. *Most [poets] are happy to be indistinguishable in public, leading quiet, domestic lives. The private aspects of the wild and the unique are saved for the poems.*

Michael VAN WALLEGHEN (1938, Detroit, MI) teaches English at the University of Illinois, Urbana–Champaign. *I sit down with a vague itch, a need to do something, a longing, perhaps, for some kind of beautiful thing. I don't quite know what I'm doing until I see it being done. It's a mystery.*

Walt WHITMAN (1819–1892, Brooklyn, NY) was a printer, then founded a newspaper, and in 1855 published the first edition of *Leaves of Grass*. During the Civil War, he tended to soldiers in the hospitals in Washington, D.C. He kept revising *Leaves of Grass* in successive editions until the deathbed edition in 1892. *To have great poets, there must be great audiences, too.*

Miller WILLIAMS (1930, Hoxie, AR) taught college biology and comparative literature. He is the father of singer-songwriter Lucinda Williams. He read his poem "History and Hope" at the inauguration of Bill Clinton in 1997. *I wrote it sitting on a big leather chair in my office with my feet on a big footstool and my dog—a little Shih Tzu named Bubba—on the footstool between my feet, a CD of John Coltrane on the stereo, and a yellow legal pad on my lap. No one asked to look at it before I read it.*

Cecilia WOLOCH (1956, Pittsburgh, PA) lives in Los Angeles, where she conducts poetry workshops in prisons, public schools and hospitals. Her blog appears at ceciliawoloch.com. *When attempting to write a prose poem—at least at the initial stages of composition— I'm trying first of all to subvert my own assumptions, saying to myself, "Oh, this is just going to be a paragraph, not a poem, and it can go in any direction."*

Gary YOUNG (1951, California) is a master letterpress printer and lives with his wife and sons in Santa Cruz, California, in a house he built himself. *I do believe that every poem is a prayer, and Saint Anthony offers a profound conundrum to the religious, and by extension, to the artist: can a monk set out to pray and then forget he is praying? Can a poet forget that he or she is writing and still write? The problem lies with the ego and with intention: I want my prayer to be perfect, my poem to be perfect, but I must somehow forget that's what I've set out to accomplish. This job is easier for saints than for the rest of us.*

Paul ZIMMER (1934, Canton, OH) ran university presses at Pittsburgh, Georgia and Iowa, and helped start the Pitt Poetry Series before he retired to write from his farm in Wisconsin. He has written more than a dozen collections of poetry. *After the Fire: A Writer Finds His Place* was published in 2002. *I urge this upon young poets when they ask me: Be patient with your careers and with your poems. It is fatal to rush the process.*

Author Index

Title Index

Permissions